Weaning Made Easy

All you need to know about spoon-feeding
and baby-led weaning – get the best of
both worlds

Dr Rana Conway (PhD, RPHNutr)

white
LADDER

Important note

The information in this book is not intended as a substitute for medical advice. Neither the author nor White Ladder can accept any responsibility for any injuries, damages or losses suffered as a result of following the information herein.

Weaning Made Easy: All you need to know about spoon-feeding and baby-led weaning – get the best of both worlds

This first edition published in 2011 by Crimson Publishing, a division of Crimson Business Ltd., Westminster House, Kew Road, Richmond, Surrey TW9 2ND

© Rana Conway 2011

British Library Cataloguing in Publication Data
A catalogue record for this book is available from the British Library

ISBN 978 1 90541 069 9

Designed by Andy Prior
Typeset by IDSUK (Data Connection) Ltd
Printed and bound in the UK by Bell and Bain Ltd., Glasgow

Contents

Contents

About the author

Rana Conway is a Registered Public Health Nutritionist and a member of the Nutrition Society. Over the past 18 years she has established herself as an expert in nutrition for pregnancy and childhood. She has carried out nutrition research at leading universities and her work with pregnant women earned her a PhD in 1997.

Rana has also lectured on a wide range of undergraduate courses and has taught nutrition to medical students, midwives and trainee dietitians. As well as writing books and research papers, Rana is the nutrition expert for *Practical Parenting & Pregnancy* magazine and writes for the NCT.

She lives in London with her husband and their three children.

Acknowledgements

Thank you to Beth Bishop at Crimson Publishing for all her ideas and enthusiasm. Also to Jane Graham Maw and Jennifer Christie at Graham Maw Christie for all their help. A big thank you to all the mums and dads who talked to me about weaning their babies. Their honesty has really helped to show how feeding a baby can be fun and rewarding but also stressful and emotional, in a way I could never have explained. Also thank you to Jenny Gordon from the Royal College of Nursing, Su Taylor from the Vegetarian Society, Kate Newman and Nicola Walpole from Coeliac UK, and Reagan Chambers from Allergy UK. Thank you too to Jenny Luigs for taking a flattering photo of me for the cover. And lastly, thank you to my husband Olly for all his help and support.

Introduction

Weaning should be an enjoyable time for both you and your baby, and should start your child on the road to a lifetime of healthy eating. But starting your child on solids can seem very daunting, especially if you're a first-time parent.

Over the past few years there have been plenty of stories in the press, all giving different advice about the best time to start weaning and which method to use. It may have left you wondering how on earth you, a busy parent, are supposed to decide, when even the experts can't agree. In fact, professional opinion isn't as divided as the media makes out, and the guidelines don't really keep changing.

One of the biggest choices you'll face when starting to wean your baby is deciding which method to use. Perhaps you're surprised to hear that there's more than one way of doing it, or perhaps you're well versed in the debates that go on in many online parenting forums and among your friends.

The big question is: do you give your baby purées and follow a traditional weaning approach, or do you try baby-led weaning and let her feed herself from the word go? This can be a confusing and controversial subject, and perhaps your friends and family are all asking you what you're going to do. Do you know what your answer is?

I'll guide you through this decision and present to you all the things you need to consider. We'll look at the pros and cons of both the traditional and baby-led weaning methods, the thinking behind them and the experiences of parents who have been through it. You'll also see that it is possible to have the best of both worlds.

Weaning made easy is designed to bring you practical, realistic advice and all the facts you need to make an informed decision. There are down-to-earth suggestions to take you through all the stages of weaning, from your baby's very first meal to the time when she can eat the same as you, and all your potential weaning worries will be answered – from fear of choking to how to stop your child becoming a fussy eater.

Introduction

While weaning can be a stressful time, it doesn't have to be. Remember, your baby is unique, and, above all, you know what's right for your baby. So take the advice, but listen to your instincts as a parent too.

I wish you every weaning success!

Rana

Author's note

For consistency and ease of reading I have referred to all babies as girls throughout. All the information applies equally to boys and no difference between boys and girls is implied.

Part one

Baby-led weaning and purées: make it work for you

In Part one, we bring you the basics of weaning. You'll find out when to start your baby on solids and what you can and can't give her to eat. We'll also look at *how* to wean your baby, and cover the two different approaches to weaning: spoon-feeding with purées and baby-led weaning (BLW) in detail.

Armed with the facts, you can work out which method suits your baby best. We'll also consider how a mixed approach can work, and what may be right for your baby.

1

The basics

To start with, let's look at the basics of weaning. This chapter contains the essential information you'll need to know to start introducing solids, regardless of the method you decide to use, or whether you are breastfeeding or giving your baby formula milk.

> 66 I was a bit apprehensive about starting solids. It seemed a big deal to be putting anything in my baby's mouth, other than milk. I started when she was exactly six months old and I followed all the advice, because I didn't have the confidence to do anything else. She was definitely ready – she was having six full (240ml) bottles of milk a day! 99
> **Sophie, mum to Ruby, 23 months**

Knowing how to go about weaning and understanding what foods to offer your baby will help make the introduction of solids as stress-free as possible for you both. You will be able to feel confident that what you're doing now will bring your baby a host of benefits. Having a good diet right from the start brings immediate health advantages and will help protect your child from the most common diet-related problems – such as anaemia, vitamin D deficiency and tooth decay, which are all too common in the first couple of years of life.

As well as affecting her immediate health, what your baby eats in these early years will also have an impact on her well-being for years to come. An increasing amount of evidence is emerging about the long-term effects of early diet. What a baby or young child eats influences her chances of suffering from obesity, raised blood pressure and heart disease in later life. We'll be looking at this in more detail later, but we're going to start with a much simpler question...

What is weaning?

Weaning is the introduction of solids into a baby's diet. It is a gradual process, which involves slowly introducing a range of foods, until she is eating the same things as the rest of the family.

The word 'weaning' is sometimes used to describe reducing milk intake and eventually stopping breastfeeding or formula altogether. In practice, the amount of milk your baby has *should* decrease as she begins to have more solid foods. However, weaning in this book refers *only* to the introduction of solids. This should happen alongside continued breastfeeding or bottle-feeding until your baby reaches her first birthday.

66 *When we started weaning we had no idea what we were doing. We expected Conrad would start solids at about six months, but it took us a while to get going and he really started at seven months. We didn't rush him. We just tried different things and gave him one new food at a time. But by eight months, he was eating pretty much whatever we had.* 99
Cory, dad to Conrad, 12 months

When to start

The question of *when* to begin introducing solids doesn't have a simple answer, unfortunately. In the past few years, the official advice appears to have changed from 'four months' to 'at least six months' and then back again. So what is going on?

To work it out, we'll look at the official guidelines from the World Health Organization (WHO) and the Department of Health (DoH), and unpick the reasoning behind their guidance. You'll then have the knowledge to be able to decide what's best for your baby, and be able to interpret official guidance appropriately.

Current guidelines and debate

The WHO recommends that, in general, babies should receive only breast milk for the first six months of life. These guidelines were issued in 2001 as part of the WHO *global* strategy for feeding infants and young children. Most experts agree that, in developing countries, exclusive breastfeeding is the best option. This is because hygiene levels are often poor, so any alternative increases a baby's risk of gastroenteritis (vomiting and diarrhoea). In these countries, infant milk and weaning foods may be of poor quality, and they are likely to have been prepared in very different conditions to those we have here. In recognition of the fact that some babies are bottle-fed already, the WHO set the same guidelines for them – bottle-fed babies should receive only formula until they are about six months old.

At the time when the WHO issued these guidelines, the recommendation from the DoH in the UK was that 'the majority of infants should not be given solid foods before the age of four months, and a mixed diet should be offered by the age of six months' (DoH, 1994). However, this advice was misinterpreted by many health professionals and parents. They thought it meant that weaning should begin at four months (16 weeks). And because they saw four months as some kind of deadline, many started earlier. In 2000, about 85% of babies in the UK were given solid food before they reached four months of age.

66 *My children started on solids much sooner than they do today and they were fine. My grandchild Stephanie was a big baby and I think she was ready for weaning early: she was always biting her fists. But her mum insisted on waiting until she was five months old.* **99**
Jane, mum of two grown-up children and granny and carer for Stephanie, 8 months

When the new WHO guidelines came out in 2001, there was a lot of debate about whether babies in developed countries such as the UK really needed to wait until six months. Many argued that babies needed more than just milk by that age and that this fact had even been mentioned in the WHO report. The WHO had acknowledged that delaying weaning until six months could lead to nutrient deficiencies, including iron deficiency in some infants, which seemed contradictory. Remember that the WHO gives global guidance.

Essentially the argument went like this: in developing countries, where vomiting and diarrhoea, resulting from poor hygiene, can be fatal, the risks of introducing solids at four or five months probably outweigh the risks of not being weaned (anaemia, for example). So weaning should wait. However, in developed countries such as the UK, the threat of illness resulting from unhygienic weaning conditions is significantly lower, so weaning before six months could be beneficial.

When you see the debate in this way, it may make the decision easier for you – and explain why the WHO appears to be very cautious about weaning.

In the UK, the DoH considered the 2001 WHO guidelines, and the fact that, at that time, 85% of babies in Britain were being weaned earlier than the recommended four to six months. In 2003, the DoH issued new guidelines recommending exclusive breastfeeding for the first six months of a baby's life and stating that six months is the recommended age for the introduction of solids for all infants, including those on formula milk.

Weaning before four months

Health professionals and experts all agree that babies should not be given foods other than milk before they are four months old. Weaning earlier than this has been associated with excessive weight gain, increased risk of infection and increased risk of allergies.

The DoH made it clear that weaning before four months was not advisable. However, just as the WHO had done, the DoH recommended that each baby (older than four months) should be managed individually. If you think your baby is ready to start on solids before six months, you will be reassured to know that even in the official 2003 recommendation it says that "all infants are individuals and will require a flexible approach". It goes on to say that if a baby is showing signs of being ready to start solids before six months (sitting up, taking an interest in other people eating and picking up and tasting food), then she should be encouraged.

> ❝ When Marcel was about four months old he became less settled and hungrier. I was breastfeeding and I had to feed him more often. This meant if his dad took him out, they could only go for a couple of hours before he needed me again. And if he saw his dad eating he would actually cry. So it seemed time to start. ❞
> **Hana, mum to Marcel, 11 months**

The media reported the new guidelines as a big turnaround in policy, leading some people to overreact and misinterpret them. Whereas parents had taken four months as the deadline to *start* weaning before the new guidelines, now they assumed six months was the absolute minimum age for any solids at all for any baby. This is the position taken by some advocates of baby-led weaning (BLW) (see p50).

In fact, the DoH guidelines say: "Six months is the recommended age for the introduction of solid foods for infants." They also state: "There are nutritional and developmental reasons why infants need solid food from six months. Infants need more iron and other nutrients than milk alone can provide."

In other words, at six months, babies need food. Since the guidelines changed in 2003, the number of babies weaned before four months has dropped from 85% to about 50%. The other half are weaned between four and six months. Less than 1% of parents breastfeed exclusively for six months.

> ❝ The others started on solids between four and six months, but Ettie seemed fine and I couldn't be bothered with the faff! But at seven months the doctor told me to. I can understand first-time mums carefully following the books, but you need to follow your instinct about when to start. ❞
> **Roberta, mum to Seb, 9 years, Benji, 4 years, Freddie, 2 years and Ettie, 18 months**

The bottom line

Start weaning when you feel it is right, with one proviso: your baby must be at least four months old. It is also sensible not to wait beyond six months.

The guidelines are there to help, but you know your baby better than anyone. If you find you get pressure from your mother, mother-in-law or health visitor, try to ignore it. Likewise, if other babies the same age have already started weaning, but you don't think your baby is quite ready, try to resist. It is not a competition, although it may sometimes feel like one. If you do start before six months, see the list of foods to stay away from until your baby is six months old (see p23). If your baby was premature, see p230 for extra information about when to start.

> **TIP** Remember that weaning your baby is something to be enjoyed, not stressed over. So relax and take it at your baby's pace.

What's right for you and your baby

In reality, lots of factors influence the decision about when to wean. There are many reasons why mums and dads choose to start weaning their baby before six months. Some think their baby is hungry, perhaps because she's crying more or waking in the night. Others say their baby seems to be more interested in food: watching them eat, grabbing from their plate, dribbling and chewing things.

There are also those who feel the sooner they get on with it, the more time there is to get weaning right. There is certainly some sense in this belief. If you wait until six months, then find your baby doesn't take much for the first few weeks, and perhaps gets a cold and goes off the whole idea completely, then you could find yourself in a situation where your baby's nutritional needs aren't being met. If you start at around five months instead, you can take it very slowly and there is no pressure on your baby. Equally, if you want to wait until six months, you shouldn't feel pressured into starting early just because others have begun weaning.

66 *I started weaning Oliver when he was five months, but he wasn't interested. I was a bit over-keen to start puréeing pears etc. and it was frustrating when I made food but he didn't eat it. I suppose it was my own fault for starting too soon. This time I'll wait until six months and hopefully it'll be easier.* 99
Rebecca, mum to Oliver, 2 years and Florence, 4 months

Is your baby ready?

Your baby may show the following signs that she is ready to begin weaning. She may:

- hold up her head unsupported
- sit well with support
- seem unsatisfied after a milk feed
- try to put toys and other things in her mouth
- reach and grab objects accurately
- watch you eat
- make chewing motions.

If your baby is showing signs that she's ready for weaning before six months, you may like to talk to your health visitor before starting. Some parents notice their baby starts waking up in the night between about three and five months and take this as a sign she needs more food. However, this is quite normal and introducing solids is unlikely to help her sleep better. If you think your baby is hungrier, she may be having a growth spurt. If she's not yet four months, or isn't showing the signs that she's developmentally ready, then give more breastfeeds or formula for the moment.

66 *Starting weaning is a big decision – it feels very much like their future health depends on it! When I had Morgan the advice had changed from four to six months, which is really hard to achieve. At four months I was breastfeeding every 1.5 to two hours in the day. I was too worried to give baby rice because of all the publicity so I switched to formula then started weaning at five months. I felt very guilty because I hadn't been able to achieve the goal set.* 99
Alice, mum to Gwen, 10 years, Evan, 8 years and Morgan, 2 years

> ## Thickening bottles – don't do it
>
> If your baby is under six months, you may not feel ready to start weaning but instead are considering putting cereal into milk feeds. This is most often done for babies who seem particularly hungry, to keep them satisfied and help them sleep through the night. However, putting cornmeal, semolina, rusks or the commercial cereal Cerelac into bottles is *not* recommended. It isn't good for growing teeth and it could result in choking.

Equipment

Buying some basic equipment before you start weaning will make things easier all round. You don't need much, but a highchair and some bibs are essential. Even if you start feeding your baby on your lap, you'll want to move on to a highchair to allow greater independence, and to make cleaning up easier.

In the early days, a **Bumbo seat** is a great piece of equipment to have. It helps babies sit up before they are able to do so confidently themselves. You can get them from almost any shop selling baby equipment and on amazon.co.uk. They are made from a kind of solid foam, and look a bit like a big potty, but they go up around the baby and have a bit between the legs. They don't have any straps and are very easy to clean, either in the sink or in the shower. They have a tray that fixes on too.

Highchairs with a tray are good for the period when your baby is exploring and smearing food everywhere. A wide tray with a rim will allow your baby to feed herself without dropping quite so much on the floor. You can then remove the tray from the highchair (get a detachable one) when your little one is about 12 to 18 months. Then your baby can still sit safely, but also enjoy being at the dinner table with the rest of the family.

Messing around

Talk to any parent about weaning and the first thing they exclaim is 'oh the mess!'.

Mess is an inevitable part of weaning, but there are things you can do to minimise the amount of time spent cleaning up.

- **A suitable bib:** either get a few that can go in the washing machine, or one that can be washed in the sink when you are cleaning up after a meal. Try different kinds to see what suits you and your baby. Some babies need a bib that goes down to their wrists; others might not like the feel of a stiff bib around their neck.

- **A floor covering:** you might want to get something to cover the floor around the highchair, especially if you have a carpet. You can get a splash mat or use an old towel or some newspaper.

- **A hand-held vacuum cleaner:** this is great for doing a quick clean-up at the end of a meal.

You'll also need some **feeding bowls and spoons** if you're going to use purées. There are quite a lot of ergonomically designed tools for babies to use to feed themselves. However, these can be rather expensive and may not make the job any easier than ordinary-shaped spoons. If a baby can use a specially designed spoon, she can usually handle a simple plastic one too.

TIP Don't give your baby metal spoons to use, as they tend to have sharper edges that could hurt your baby's gums if she bites down on them.

If you're planning to make purées or even if you're going to try BLW, a **hand-held blender** is wonderful. You can use it to make fruit and vegetable purées, if you're starting that way, but it's also good for creating dips and soups.

You'll also need some **ice-cube trays or little pots** for storing food in the freezer. Cooking in bulk and freezing is useful for both purées and BLW. Freezer bags and a permanent marker pen will also come in handy, as it can be hard to identify baby food once it's frozen!

> TIP Some more traditional weaning guides recommend buying specialist baby food mills or grinders – these aren't really necessary as you'll use them for only a few months and they don't really have any advantage over a hand-held blender.

Equipment checklist

- Highchair – with removable tray
- Bibs
- Bowls
- Spoons
- Blender
- Ice-cube tray and pots
- Freezer bags
- Permanent marker pen

What should your baby eat?

A healthy diet for a baby involves the right balance of foods from the five food groups.

- **Starchy foods**, such as bread, pasta and potatoes, provide babies with energy. For adults, it is best to have wholemeal bread and brown rice and pasta, but these can be too bulky for babies, so a mixture of these and white rice and pasta is best.
- **Protein foods**, including meat, fish, eggs and lentils, contain the amino acids needed for growth. These foods also supply iron and zinc as well as other vitamins and minerals. A healthy diet contains a variety of different protein-rich foods.
- **Milk and dairy foods** supply your baby with calcium for strong bones and teeth.
- **Fruit and vegetables** reduce the risk of many adult diseases, including stroke, heart disease and some cancers. They also supply babies with many essential vitamins and minerals, as well as fibre, which is needed to prevent constipation. Offering a good variety of different-coloured fruits and vegetables (green, orange, red, yellow, etc.) is a good way of ensuring your baby gets the benefits of all the different vitamins, minerals and phytochemicals they provide.
- **Foods containing fat and sugar** should be kept to a minimum in

adult diets, but babies need more fat than us to ensure they have or enough calories, essential fatty acids and fat-soluble vitamins (vitamins A, D and E). They should get all they need by eating oily fish, full-fat dairy foods and a mixture of different oils and spreads, including olive oil and rapeseed oil. They don't need fatty foods like sausages and cakes, although it's fine to have these occasionally.

TIP When giving your child dairy products, remember that children should have full-fat milk, yogurt and cheese until they are at least two years old.

Giving your baby a balanced diet means including foods from all the food groups in her diet. This is the best way of ensuring she gets all the nutrients she needs. Moving from milk to a balanced diet may seem like an enormous change, but don't worry – it happens very gradually.

At the start of weaning you'll only be serving fruit and vegetables, and your baby will still be getting most of her nutrients from breast milk or formula. As you introduce more foods, you'll find she takes less milk. In Part two we'll go step by step through the process from the first mouthful to toddlerhood. You'll learn about the best foods to give your baby at each stage and see why it will be some time yet before she's ready to eat the same food as you.

As well as the main food groups, there are other things you should be aware of, which we'll go through below. These might all seem like unnecessary extras to worry about – but they can boost your child's health very easily and are proven to be extremely beneficial.

Essential minerals and vitamins

For optimal health, babies need a diet packed with all the essential vitamins and minerals. The meal plans included in Part two have been designed to provide the right balance of vitamins and minerals.

Mineral	Where is it found?	What is it for?
Iron	Meat, fish, eggs, potatoes and fortified breakfast cereals	Healthy red blood cells – if babies do not get enough they can become anaemic
Calcium	Milk, cheese and yogurt Green vegetables also have a small amount	Healthy bones and teeth and blood-clotting
Zinc	Meat, milk, eggs, wholegrain cereals, nuts and pulses	Growth, a healthy immune system and healing of wounds

Vitamin	Where is it found?	What is it for?
Vitamin A	In liver and oily fish, as retinol, and as beta-carotene in carrots, apricots and pumpkins	Eye development, healthy skin and a good immune system
Vitamin B1 (thiamin)	Wholegrain cereals and fortified breakfast cereals, salmon, tuna and beans	Releasing energy from food
Folic acid	Oranges, leafy green vegetables and fortified breakfast cereals	Making new cells
Vitamin B12	Meat, fish, eggs and milk products Also added to some vegetarian foods	Making new cells
Vitamin C	Oranges, strawberries, kiwi fruit, broccoli, cabbage and potatoes	Helping iron absorption and also important for healing and healthy gums
Vitamin D	Oily fish, eggs and dairy products The main source is sunlight on the skin	Helping calcium absorption and ensuring healthy bones – deficiency can result in rickets
Vitamin E	Vegetable oils, wholegrain cereals, nuts and leafy green vegetables	An anti-oxidant and protects against cancer and heart disease

What you can do about iron deficiency

During weaning, babies are particularly vulnerable to iron deficiency or anaemia, because the iron stores they were born with have diminished and many don't yet eat enough iron-rich foods. A recent survey in the UK suggested that anaemia affects around 20% of babies.

Researchers in the US found that babies who were exclusively breastfed for six months were more likely to develop anaemia than those weaned at four or five months.

Iron deficiency affects motor development and may also be associated with delays in mental and social development. To prevent it, babies need to have iron-rich foods such as meat, fish, eggs, potatoes, vegetables and fortified cereals.

The amount of iron absorbed increases when foods rich in vitamin C are eaten at the same time. So your baby will be able to get more iron from her breakfast cereal if you give her fruit with a high level of vitamin C, such as strawberries or kiwi fruit, at the same time.

> 66 I started weaning all three of mine between four and five months – partly because I would have had to breastfeed them almost constantly if I hadn't, but also because at six months babies need food. I wanted to have enough time to be able to do it gradually. It worries me when people start at six months and then take their time and introduce one food at a time. At six months, babies need to start eating lumps and iron-rich foods almost straight away. 99
> **Gail, dietitian and mum to Rory, 11 years, Aidan, 8 years and Oscar, 5 years**

Do you need to use vitamin drops?

The DoH recommends drops containing vitamins A, C and D for babies from six months until they reach five years of age. This applies to all babies unless they are drinking more than 500ml of formula milk each day (formula has vitamin D added to it already).

The drops are especially important for babies with darker skin (such as those of African-Caribbean and South Asian origin). This is because we get most of our vitamin D naturally when our skin is exposed to sunlight, and people with darker skin need more sunlight to get enough of the vitamin. Although vitamin D can be found in some foods, it is only in a limited number, such as oily fish and fortified margarine.

> TIP There is no need to buy an expensive brand of vitamin drops. But you must get supplements that are specifically for babies, and not give them more than one type at a time.

Oily fish and omega 3 fatty acids

Oily fish, such as salmon and sardines, contain omega 3 fatty acids, which are important for good health. You may also have noticed the term 'omega 3s' on lots of other food products, including margarine, mayonnaise and even bread. Another term, 'LCPs' is also used to describe these beneficial fatty acids, and you may have spotted this on formula. If you're unsure exactly what the terms mean or why these fatty acids are important for babies, then going back to basics will help.

There are two types of omega 3s: short-chain omega 3s, which are found in seeds (e.g. linseed oil) and long-chain omega 3s, which are found in oily fish (e.g. salmon). These long-chain omega 3s are basically the same thing as long-chain polyunsaturates (LCPs), and it is these that are beneficial. Unfortunately, the long chemical names and initials don't make the topic any easier to understand!

> TIP If you see a product with added omega 3s, check whether it really contains long-chain omega 3s, which are vital for your baby's brain and eye development. It may just contain short-chain omega 3s, which don't have the same health benefits.

LCPs are vital for a baby's development, with one type alone making up 25% of the brain's fatty acids. The first year of life sees rapid development in a baby's brain, so a good intake of LCPs is especially important during this time. LCPs also play a role in the development of vision – they make up 50% of fatty acids in the retina. Several trials have looked at improving the LCP intake of babies and have found that higher intakes are linked with improved mental development and better visual clarity.

Unfortunately, few babies and toddlers seem to be getting all the benefits LCPs can offer. Only 14% of pre-schoolers in the UK eat oily fish, which suggests that 86% are unlikely to have a good LCP intake. Health messages about getting your '5 a day' are well known, but campaigns promoting the benefits of oily fish haven't been so successful.

According to a poll of parents about fish consumption, about one in five children don't like fish. But why aren't the other four-fifths eating it? Some parents say they're put off cooking fish by the smell, others are concerned their children might choke on the bones.

There are also those who argue that fish is full of pollution and therefore dangerous. This comes from the fact that some oily fish can contain pollutants, such as mercury. The level of these pollutants is measured regularly, and mercury has been found in relatively high quantities in some fish, such as swordfish (see p28), so these species should not be eaten by babies. However, when it comes to fish such as salmon and mackerel, the potential harm from pollutants has to be weighed up against the benefits from the omega 3s they contain. Fears about harmful chemicals in fish are relatively new, but in fact the levels of pollutants in fish have fallen by 75% in the past 20 years.

> TIP Men and boys can eat up to four portions of oily fish a week. Women and girls (who may one day become pregnant) can eat two portions a week. By eating this amount, the health benefits outweigh any possible risks from pollutants.

All of these concerns are understandable, but making the effort to get the whole family eating oily fish is worthwhile – even if it's just once a week. It isn't just important for your baby's brain development, but also for the immune system and, as you get older, for the health of your eyes, brain and heart.

The wonders of phytochemicals

The importance of phytochemicals is a relatively new discovery. The word 'phytochemical' basically means a chemical from a plant, but it is now used to describe substances in plant-based foods that have health benefits. 'Superfoods' (blueberries or pomegranates, for example) are so-called because of the phytochemicals they contain. By eating a range of different-coloured fruits and vegetables, your baby will get a variety of the different, wonderful phytochemicals.

Research is continuing into the health benefits of phytochemicals, but these include playing a protective role against cancer and reducing the risk of asthma.

This is another great reason to encourage your baby to grow up eating fruit and vegetables (if you needed another one). Multivitamin and mineral supplements, and foods with added vitamin C or other vitamins, are sometimes seen as a substitute for fruit and vegetables. But while they may include nutrients such as vitamin C, they don't contain the wide range of phytochemicals found in fruit and vegetables, so they don't offer all the health benefits of the real thing.

> 66 *A friend gave me a really good tip – cook up some frozen chopped veg (carrots and corn, etc.) and put them in a pot to take with you when you're going out and about. It works really well as a snack and it's so easy. Evan loves it and it's much healthier than giving him the crisps and other snacks that are available for babies his age.* 99
> **Sam, mum to Callum, 4 years and Evan, 10 months**

Probiotics and prebiotics

Probiotics are live micro-organisms that are beneficial to health. They are also known as 'friendly bacteria'. Yogurt contains probiotics, and specific strains are now found in a number of yogurt drinks, including some for children.

Prebiotics are simply the food that probiotics eat. Prebiotics aren't digested directly, but eating more of them helps the beneficial micro-organisms in your intestines to multiply. Prebiotics are found naturally in some foods, including bananas, leeks and raw oats. They are also added to some processed foods such as breakfast cereal.

Probiotics can be helpful when babies and toddlers are suffering from diarrhoea, helping them to get better quicker. They may be particularly useful when a baby is taking a course of antibiotics, as these can disrupt the normal balance of bacteria in the intestines. Probiotics and prebiotics have also been linked to other health benefits, including improving constipation, colds and colic.

What about drinks?

When you start weaning, it's important to offer your baby a cup of water with each meal. She should also have one available for whenever she wants it.

For babies younger than six months, water should be boiled and cooled. This isn't necessary for older babies.

> TIP Mineral water and other bottled waters may not be suitable for babies because of the high mineral content. If you have to use bottled water, look for one that is labelled as suitable for babies, or one that contains less than 200mg of sodium per litre.

Babies and children aren't as sensitive to thirst as adults, and some go for long periods without drinking. Even when they've been very active or the weather is hot, they might not realise they need a drink. You may notice them displaying signs of dehydration, including confusion, irritability and lethargy, even though they don't recognise how thirsty they are. That means it's important for you to remember to give them drinks regularly.

Your baby probably won't drink much water to start with, but resist giving her juice instead. Once a baby gets used to drinking juice or other alternatives, it is very hard to get her to go back to plain water. If water is the only option, she will quickly get used to it, and it is a good habit to have for life. If you really want to give juice, then dilute it one part pure fruit juice (not squash) to 10 parts water, and only give it with meals. At other times, give milk or plain water, as anything else is bad for the teeth.

> 66 *We started giving William water in a bottle because he was bottle-fed anyway so he was used to it. Then he had a cup with a spout. When it comes to choosing a cup, like other things, a lot of it is driven by how much mess you will put up with.* 99
> **Toby, dad to William, 3 years**

Choosing a cup

It is a good idea to get your baby used to drinking from a cup from about six months. It's best to get one with a lid, but choosing exactly which one to buy can be difficult.

To start with at least, get a free-flow cup. This is one without a valve – it is easier to get water out, and it will encourage sipping. Some baby cups have very strong valves, which means there's no risk of spillage, but not much chance of your baby getting anything out of it either.

When your baby is older and is used to drinking from a cup, you might want one with a valve for using around the house or when you're out, to reduce spillage, but a free-flow cup is still preferable for meal times.

Foods to avoid at different ages

However you choose to feed your baby, and whenever you start weaning, there are certain foods your baby should avoid. This will reduce the risk of allergies, choking and food poisoning and will help keep your baby healthy.

Foods to try *only* after six months

- Meat
- Fish and seafood
- Eggs
- Nuts and seeds (including peanut butter)
- Foods containing gluten, including bread, some breakfast cereals (such as Weetabix), pasta and rusks
- Dairy products, such as cows' milk, cheese and yogurt
- Beans and pulses
- Citrus fruit, such as oranges

Foods to avoid for the first year

- Honey
- Salt
- Sugar
- Whole nuts
- Low-fat foods
- High-fibre foods
- Uncooked or partly cooked eggs (e.g. soft-boiled)
- Blue and unpasteurised cheeses
- Raw shellfish
- Shark, swordfish and marlin
- Smoked and salted meats and fish
- Fizzy drinks
- Caffeine
- Cows' milk (apart from small amounts in food)

Honey

Honey shouldn't be added to food or used to ease coughs. Very occasionally, honey can contain a type of bacteria that can get into a baby's intestines and produce a toxin or poison, which leads to infant botulism (an illness that causes muscle weakness and breathing problems). Honey is safe for children over one year, but a young baby's gut is not sufficiently developed to fight off the botulism. Infant botulism is incredibly rare and there have been only 11 cases in the past 30 years. Babies usually recover fully from infant botulism, but it is a very serious illness. Hospital treatment is usually needed and recovery can be slow.

Salt

Salt contains sodium, and when babies have too much, their kidneys can't cope. Salt should *never* be added to a baby's food. You also need to be careful about other high-salt flavourings, such as stock cubes, soya sauce, gravy and cook-in sauces. When you're cooking for the whole family, avoid adding salt and choose low-salt stock cubes and sauces. That way your baby can share the same food. It will also benefit the entire family, as most of us have too much salt in our diets. Instead, you can give food more flavour by cooking with lemon juice, garlic, ginger and herbs, such as basil and parsley.

Salt guidelines

- Babies under one year should have no more than 1g of salt per day (0.4g sodium)
- One to three-year-olds should have no more than 2g per day (0.8g sodium)

Most of the salt in our diets comes from processed foods, so often we don't know we're eating it. It is important to read food labels to avoid giving your baby family foods that contain a lot of salt. Be particularly careful with products such as pasta sauces, ready meals and processed meats, like sausages. Even foods that do not taste particularly salty, such as bread and breakfast cereals, contain hidden salt. If a baby has these every day, her salt intake soon adds up. For example, a slice of toast for breakfast would mean a baby was already halfway towards the maximum daily intake. And if she had a slice of ham mixed into her dinner and a bit of ketchup, she could easily exceed the level.

> TIP Buy lower-salt versions of foods such as baked beans and ketchup.

As a rough guide, the following can help.

- Foods containing more than 1.5g salt per 100g (0.6g sodium) are considered high in salt.
- Foods containing less than 0.3g salt per 100g (0.1g sodium) are considered low in salt.

Another problem with giving babies and young children salty food is that they get used to it. Then, when they are older, they will prefer saltier foods, which generally means more processed foods. It is much better for babies to get used to having unprocessed foods, such as rice, vegetables and fish. So start your baby on healthy eating now and you'll find it easier to keep to healthy eating as she grows up.

The salt content of typical foods

Food and portion	Salt content (g)
Tomato ketchup (tablespoon)	0.3
Reduced-salt tomato ketchup (tablespoon)	Less than 0.1
Bread (one slice)	0.5
Weetabix (one)	0.1
Cheerios (30g bowl)	0.4
Cornflakes (30g bowl)	0.5
Ham (one slice)	0.4
Sausages (one)	0.5 to 1.3
Bacon (one rasher)	0.7
Salami or chorizo (one slice)	0.2
Smoked salmon (50g)	2.4

Continued over page

Continued from overleaf

Food and portion	Salt content (g)
Grilled salmon (50g)	Less than 0.1
Cheddar cheese (dice-sized cube)	0.1
Baked beans (tablespoon)	0.2
Reduced-salt baked beans (tablespoon)	0.1
Olives (each)	0.1

To calculate the sodium content of these foods, divide the salt content by 2.5 (1g of sodium is equivalent to 2.5g of salt).

> **❝** *I made special meals just for Dhiya Mary until she reached 12 months old, without any salt or spice. Now she eats the Indian food I cook for everyone and she likes spicy food. She eats lamb and lentils and everything. I only cook with a little salt then we add more when we eat, if we want.* **❞**
> **Sophia, mum to Dhiya Mary, 13 months**

Sugar

Babies do *not* need sugar! If they eat very sweet food from an early age they may suffer from tooth decay and they'll get a taste for it. Dental health may not be a concern for you at the moment, but it does affect very young children. In the last national UK survey, it was found that 17% of 1½ to 2½-year-olds had tooth decay.

Having sugary foods such as biscuits or rusks between meals increases the risk of tooth decay, as does fruit juice or squash between meals. Drinking juice from a bottle is particularly harmful as your baby is likely to keep it in her mouth for longer, which increases the time the sugar is in contact with the teeth.

Sugar provides calories but has no other nutritional value. It comes in many forms, so if you're reading food labels you should also look out for the following:

- glucose syrup
- corn syrup
- high-fructose corn syrup

- honey
- molasses
- fruit juice concentrates (e.g. grape juice concentrate)
- any word ending in 'ose' (e.g. sucrose, fructose or maltose).

Even snacks such as raisins and malt loaf can be a problem if babies have them regularly between meals and spend a long time eating them. These contain natural sugar and may well seem healthy. They are certainly healthier than most biscuits or cakes, but because they are sticky, the sugar in them stays in contact with a baby's teeth for longer. So it might be better to give raisins or other dried fruit at the end of a meal, or as a snack only a couple of times a week. This way your baby gets the benefits of the nutrients they contain, but has less risk of tooth decay. Fresh fruit also contains natural sugars, but because foods like apples and bananas contain lots of water too, the sugar doesn't stick around in the mouth for so long. Foods such as breadsticks and cheese are also good for snacking (see p90).

As babies get older they will inevitably eat more sugar, and while cakes and biscuits are fine occasionally, you don't want your child to develop a sweet tooth if it can be avoided.

> TIP If you find certain foods are too sour for your baby, for example stewed apple, then try adding mashed banana or your baby's usual milk. That way you're not just adding calories, you're also providing more vitamins and minerals.

Nuts

Whole nuts shouldn't be given to children under five years old, as they can choke on them. From six months, crushed nuts, including peanuts, can be given, as can nut butters, like peanut butter (see p23).

Low-fat foods

Low-fat foods, such as skimmed or semi-skimmed milk, low-fat yogurt, cheese or cheese spreads, are not suitable for children under two years old. This is because infants have high energy requirements relative to their size, and fats are an important source of calories.

Foods containing fat are also important for supplying fat-soluble vitamins.

High-fibre foods

Foods with added dietary fibre, such as wheat germ, All-Bran and bran flakes, are not suitable for babies. Babies have small stomachs and they are growing rapidly, so they need plenty of foods that are packed with calories and nutrients. Eating high-fibre foods can fill them up too quickly, before they've had all the calories and nutrients they need. Fibre also reduces the absorption of some nutrients, including iron and zinc. These minerals can become bound to the fibre and carried straight through the body.

Saturated fat and trans fat

Babies and children should not have too many foods that are high in saturated fat, such as butter, fatty meat, sausages and meat pies. Too much saturated fat can increase a person's cholesterol level and their risk of heart disease. Although we assume these problems really only affect adults, the damaging impact of excess saturated fat starts much earlier in life.

Trans fat is another ingredient to avoid. It is also called hydrogenated fat, or you may see the term 'partially hydrogenated' on food labels. Food manufacturers use trans fats because they are cheap and give foods a longer shelf life. They are found in foods such as biscuits, cakes, sausages and burgers.

Shark, swordfish and marlin

The Food Standards Agency recommends that these fish are not eaten by anyone under the age of 16. This is because the amount of mercury they contain could affect a child's developing nervous system.

Cows' milk

Until babies are a year old, they should have breast milk or infant formula to drink.

Cows' milk isn't suitable as a drink because the proteins it contains are difficult for a baby to digest. It also has too much sodium and not enough iron and other essential nutrients to meet a baby's needs. It can also irritate the lining of a baby's intestines.

From six months, it is OK to give small amounts of cows' milk in foods – if you are making mashed potato, for example.

Likewise, goats' and sheep's milk and drinks made from oats aren't suitable for babies under a year, as they don't contain the iron and other nutrients a baby needs.

Reduce the risk of food poisoning

To avoid the risk of food poisoning, babies should only have eggs that have been cooked until both the white and yolk are hard.

The Food Standards Agency also says that babies, along with pregnant women, are vulnerable to listeria (which can range from mild, flu-like symptoms to the risk of meningitis or pneumonia). Therefore it is best not to give your baby soft, mould-ripened cheeses, such as brie, camembert or chèvre, or blue cheeses like Stilton – which you'll have avoided throughout your pregnancy too.

Preparing food for your baby

Whatever weaning approach you decide to try, whether you decide to start with purées or to take the BLW approach and give finger foods from the beginning, there will be cooking involved. As babies are more vulnerable to food poisoning than adults, it's important to think about a few basic hygiene rules. Cross-contamination, for example from raw meat to other products, is one of the commonest causes of food poisoning, and even if you're an experienced cook, it's worth reading through the food safety checklists.

Cooking checklist

- Keep kitchen surfaces and equipment such as chopping boards clean.

- Have a separate chopping board that is used only for raw meat and fish to help prevent cross-contamination of harmful bacteria to foods like bread or fruit, which aren't cooked before eating.
- Regularly clean the inside and outside of your fridge and freezer.
- Don't allow pets near food or on work surfaces.
- Check 'use by' and 'best before' dates carefully as babies are at greater risk of food poisoning than adults.
- Check that seals on jars or bottles haven't been broken.
- Wash all fruit and salad vegetables carefully.

In an ideal world, you'd spend hours cooking each meal from scratch with fresh ingredients and then the whole family would sit down together to enjoy it. In reality this isn't always possible. To start with, the foods you eat are unlikely to be suitable for a baby who is just beginning weaning.

You also may not want to have a meal at the same time as your baby. To make things easier, many parents cook batches of food for their baby and put them in the freezer. You might find it easiest to spend a few hours in the kitchen at the weekend when you have more time. Or when you're cooking for the family, you could make extra for freezing.

> **TIP** Certain foods fare better when frozen than others. Purées freeze well and so do vegetable sticks. Other meals, such as shepherd's pie, pasta sauces and soups, also freeze well.

Storage checklist

Whenever you are planning to store food, there are some basic precautions to take.

- Raw meat and fish should be covered and placed at the bottom of the fridge so they can't drip onto other food.
- Cool food as quickly as possible (within one to two hours) and store it in the fridge or freezer. This is particularly important for foods such as meat, fish, eggs and rice, which are more likely to cause food poisoning.

- If you divide the food into smaller portions it will cool more quickly.
- Airtight containers are ideal for storage, but remember that food expands when frozen, so don't forget to leave a bit of space at the top of the container.
- Fridges should be kept between 0 and 5°C to prevent bacteria growing. Freezers should be below 18°C. It's a good idea to get a thermometer if your fridge or freezer is old, or you're not sure about its temperature.
- Food placed in the fridge should be eaten within one to two days.
- Remember to label any containers for freezing with the date and contents.
- Food placed in the freezer should generally be eaten within three months.

Reheating checklist

- Defrost food before reheating it, ideally in the fridge overnight or in the microwave on the 'defrost' setting.
- Once food is removed from the freezer it should be eaten within about 24 hours or thrown away.
- Reheat food until it is piping hot all the way through, then cool it to the right temperature for your baby. If your baby is in a hurry for dinner, you can put the bowl containing the hot meal in a larger bowl of cold water to cool it more quickly.
- Once you have reheated a meal, it should be eaten or thrown away. Never reheat food more than once.

Meal-time checklist

- Wash your and your baby's hands with soap and warm water before meals.
- Wash all bowls and spoons for feeding in hot soapy water. Equipment for meals does not need to be sterilised. This is only necessary for bottles.
- Always give food a good mix then test the temperature before giving it to your baby.
- Never leave your baby unattended when she is eating.

What you can do to stop choking

This might be one of your biggest worries when starting to wean your baby.

Babies can choke on hard foods such as raw carrot and round foods such as cherry tomatoes. And this can be scary for the parent.

To reduce the risk of this happening:

- lightly cook hard foods until your baby has enough teeth to cope with them safely
- cut foods such as cherry tomatoes and grapes in half
- be careful with foods that have skin, such as chicken and sausages, and fish with bones.

The NHS Choices website has comprehensive advice about what to do if your baby does choke (www.nhs.uk). Ensure that you are familiar with this basic first aid, as it will mean you feel more confident in feeding your baby, and are able to do something in an emergency too.

Don't worry if it seems like there is loads of information in this chapter to take in all at once. You don't need to. You'll probably find you want to refer back to much of the information during the weaning process – such as which foods contain iron or salt or other nutrients, or when you can give your baby cows' milk or other foods.

With the basics under your belt, the next thing to do is to decide on the approach you are going to take. This might sound strange, but there are options! Are you going to start weaning by giving your baby puréed food, or would you like to try baby-led weaning and offer her pieces of food to feed herself?

In the next two chapters, you'll find out about each of the two approaches: how to do it, the advantages and disadvantages, and the experiences of other parents. You may then choose to try one or the other. Alternatively, once you've read Chapter 4, 'The balanced approach', you may well decide to take the best of both worlds.

2

Purées and traditional weaning

The traditional weaning method starts with purées or mashed food. It has worked for generations and most parents are quite happy with it. It is also likely to be the route suggested by health visitors. Most books specifically about weaning, including those by Annabel Karmel and Gina Ford, also suggest starting with purées. Perhaps unsurprisingly, it is also the approach favoured by baby food companies and you'll find advice about how to do it in their leaflets and on their websites.

Some babies take to solids quickly and are happy to eat whatever they're given. Inevitably, for others it is a slower process and they may be much choosier. Advocates of baby-led weaning (BLW) have blamed the traditional approach for turning some babies into fussy eaters. The idea seems to be that only BLW babies can choose what they eat; others can't, and so they become suspicious about food, resulting in fussy eating. However, in reality the traditional approach suits many babies and their parents very well.

> 66 I started giving Filip baby rice when he was six months old, then puréed apple and pear, and vegetables like sweet potato, etc. He's always eaten well and I'm sometimes surprised that he eats things like beetroot and spinach that

I know some babies wouldn't eat. He has fish twice a week and really he eats everything I give him. I plan to do the same with Emily. **99**
Tatiana, mum to Filip, 18 months and Emily, 3 months

How it works

With traditional weaning, babies are first given baby rice or a very smooth purée of fruit or vegetables, followed by mixtures of baby rice and puréed fruit or vegetables.

Between about six and seven months, they move on to slightly lumpier purées and a wider range of foods, including meat and fish. Babies may have some finger foods too, generally for snacks, but for their main meals, they are fed with a spoon.

> TIP In practice some nine or 10-month-old babies suddenly refuse to be spoon-fed and decide they'd rather feed themselves. Others continue to be fed with a spoon well past their first birthday.

From about nine months, babies can have mashed or chopped meals, and they can start trying to feed themselves.

In the past, when the majority of babies were weaned before four months, this was really the only option. At that age, babies can't feed themselves. They are also unable to cope with anything other than a smooth purée. BLW, which involves babies feeding themselves, wasn't an option.

Now that parents are advised to wait until their baby is about six months old to begin weaning, it isn't always necessary to start with smooth purées. This is one of the reasons why a growing number of parents are deciding to follow the BLW route, and not use any purées at all. Parents who decide to start weaning before their baby is six months old usually start with purées.

How to do it

If you've read about weaning or chatted with other parents, you may already have a fair idea about what is involved in weaning with purées. However, there are different ways to go about it.

Babies can be started on purées at different ages. Some are fed only homemade food. Others have only jars, which isn't advisable and is discussed on p45. Babies who have solids between four and six months are more likely to be given commercially prepared baby food, according to the 2005 Infant Feeding Survey. Older babies are generally given more homemade foods. Many parents follow special recipes to prepare foods for weaning. Others simply take some of the foods they are cooking for the family and purée these. Using a combination of homemade food and the odd jar for convenience is also common. Some babies who start on purées move swiftly on to lumps, finger foods and family foods, while others are still having completely smooth meals for longer.

To mouli or not to mouli?

Some advocates of this weaning method believe a mouli is an essential piece of equipment.

A mouli is a type of food mill with a handle. You place food in the top and turn the handle, and the food is pushed through cutting discs to make a purée. Any skin or seeds are left behind, which is assumed to be better for babies. However, that may not be the case, as there is nutritional goodness in the skin of some fruit and vegetables.

There are lengthy online discussions about moulis, and while there seems to be a general consensus that they create the very best mashed potato, there is less agreement about their use in making baby food. Some parents find them fiddly and say they create too much washing up, but others say they couldn't manage without them. The alternative is a hand-held blender, and this is what most parents use. However, a mouli may be useful on holiday, as you don't have to plug it in.

The stages of weaning with purées

Traditional weaning guides advise parents to move through the following stages when they introduce solids. These stages may have been necessary when babies were weaned at around four months, but they are still given for babies who are being weaned later. We'll look at whether this one-size-fits-all approach is really appropriate for all babies in Chapter 4. However, it certainly works for some and it's useful to look at what happens at each stage.

1. Introducing baby rice

Traditional weaning usually begins when babies are between four and six months old. The first food they are given is generally baby rice – fine powdery rice flakes that can be mixed with milk or water. Baby rice is fortified with thiamin (vitamin B1), which enables the body to convert carbohydrates into energy. Thiamin is usually found in the outer coating of rice, but is lost when rice is refined to produce white rice or baby rice. So it is simply added back into baby rice via fortification, to act as a safeguard against deficiency. When baby rice is made up it has a very bland taste, not that different to milk, which is why it is given first.

The baby rice is mixed with your baby's usual milk, either breast milk or formula. At the beginning you add just a small amount of baby rice, but this increases over the next few days.

2. Introducing purées

After giving baby rice for between two and seven days, you start introducing some fruit or vegetables. Pear or carrot purée is usually given first, as these are quite sweet and tend to be fairly popular with babies. Only one new food is introduced at a time so that it is easier to pinpoint the cause if a baby has an allergic reaction. At this stage, babies have food at one meal every day so they can get used to it.

Guidelines for babies of different ages aren't usually set out, but in Chapter 6 we'll look at why older babies should move on more quickly.

Some people prefer to start with puréed fruit or vegetables rather than baby rice and this is fine. If your baby is six months old when you begin, there is really no need to start with baby rice or to take things so slowly.

> TIP The advice for introducing solids is often presented as one standard method, but really it should be tailored according to your baby's age and stage of development.

3. Increasing the amount and variety of purées

After a few different purées have been introduced, progress is faster.

Over the next few weeks you can make the following changes.

- Gradually give the food a thicker consistency.
- Make vegetable purées more substantial by adding potato or yam, or mixing them with baby rice.
- Slowly increase the amount of food you offer at each meal.
- Gradually increase the number of meals your baby has each day from one to two and then three. Some people suggest babies have four meals each day: breakfast, lunch, tea and supper.
- Increase the variety of foods.

The meal plan below shows the type of foods typically suggested for a baby who has been taking solids for a few weeks and has progressed to three meals a day. Some babies may still have a breastfeed or a bottle of formula at lunchtime, but this feed is usually dropped once babies reach three meals a day. The other breast or bottle feeds are still important at this stage.

A traditional meal plan for a five to six-month-old baby

Day	Morning	Mid-morning	Lunch	Mid-afternoon	Tea time	Bedtime
Day 1	Milk feed Fruit compote	Milk feed	Carrot and potato purée	Milk feed	Cream of fruit with baby rice	Milk feed
Day 2	Milk feed Baby cereal	Milk feed	Courgette, watercress and potato purée	Milk feed	Peach and mango purée	Milk feed
Day 3	Milk feed Banana porridge	Milk feed	Broccoli and cauliflower purée with baby rice	Milk feed	Apple and pear purée	Milk feed

Water should be offered with all meals.

If you compare this with the advice in Chapter 6 (see p114), you'll notice that there are different plans depending on your baby's age when you start weaning – something that traditional weaning guides don't usually take into account.

4. Six months – starting new foods

Once your baby is six months old, you start giving protein-rich foods such as meat, fish, eggs and lentils. These can be puréed along with vegetables and carbohydrate foods such as breakfast cereal, potatoes, rice and pasta.

From six or seven months you also start to introduce some finger foods.

5. Introducing lumps

When your baby is between six and eight months, it's time for her to move on from smooth purées to lumpier foods. If you're buying jars or pots of baby food, then you can start getting 'stage 2' meals now (as you'll see on the label). If you've been making purées yourself, then start mashing meals instead of using a blender.

The meal plan below shows the type of meals that are typically suggested for babies of this age. You'll notice that every day there are two proper cooked meals. It is usually suggested that each of these meals is prepared using a special weaning recipe or is bought ready-made. Dishes are sometimes similar to those eaten by adults, but there are also some (such as haddock in orange sauce) that adults wouldn't usually eat.

In Chapter 7, we'll show you that babies can get all the nutrients they need from a much simpler menu.

A traditional meal plan for a seven to nine-month-old baby

Day	Morning	Mid-morning	Lunch	Mid-afternoon	Tea time	Bedtime
Day 1	Milk feed Weetabix with mashed banana	Rice cakes	Macaroni cheese Grated apple	Milk feed Half a banana	Spaghetti bolognaise Fruit jelly	Milk feed
Day 2	Milk feed Baby cereal with fruit purée	Breadsticks and cheese	Chicken and apricot casserole Baked banana	Milk feed Toast fingers	Haddock in orange sauce Banana custard	Milk feed
Day 3	Milk feed Scrambled egg with toast fingers	Half a banana	Beef stew Fruit salad	Milk feed Ham and pitta bread	Lentil and vegetable bake Peach yogurt	Milk feed

Water should be offered with all meals and snacks.

6. Moving on from purées

Between nine months and a year, babies should move from mashed meals to chopped or minced family meals. As well as having three meals a day, two snacks are provided for extra energy.

A traditional meal plan for a 10 to 12-month-old baby

Day	Morning	Mid-morning	Lunch	Mid-afternoon	Tea time	Bedtime
Day 1	Milk feed Porridge	Banana	Tuna pasta bake Apple and raspberry purée	Milk feed Baby biscuit	Fruity rice with chicken Apple crumble	Milk feed
Day 2	Milk feed French toast	Breadsticks	Lamb casserole Yogurt	Milk feed Vegetable sticks and houmous	Fish pie Baked apple and custard	Milk feed
Day 3	Milk feed Blueberry pancakes	Sliced kiwi	Vegetable and chickpea curry Rice pudding	Milk feed Toast fingers and cheese	Shepherd's pie Fruit salad	Milk feed

Water should be offered with all meals and snacks.

In the meal plan above you'll notice that there are still at least two proper cooked meals a day. In Chapter 8 (see p159) you'll see an alternative meal plan for babies of this age. The meals here have all the ingredients mixed together, but it's good for babies to get used to handling and tasting different foods, such as broccoli or raspberries, on their own.

> 66 I've never followed any recipes for Noah, I've just cooked what I had and I thought would be appropriate. I've heard the advice about family meals being best but I find it difficult to cook when he's around and by the time my husband gets home from work Noah's in bed. I sometimes cook simple meals just for him, or when I'm cooking our dinner I'll take some out for him for the next day, before I add spices or anything like that. 99
> **Elisabeth, mum to Noah, 14 months**

We'll now have a look at the advantages and disadvantages of purées. Many fans of BLW feel very strongly against this traditional approach, and you may have heard arguments against it. Here we give you a balanced look at the pros and cons, to help you make up your own mind.

The advantages of purées

Slower developers can still eat

One clear advantage of purées over BLW is that it doesn't rely on a baby's food-handling skills. You can give a baby purée before she is capable of picking up food, getting it to her mouth and chewing.

Baby-led weaners (BLWers) argue that babies don't need solids until they are able to feed themselves. However, that argument would imply that bottle-fed babies who can't hold their own bottle don't need milk, which no one would agree with!

BLWers also appear to interpret the official advice as meaning that six months is the minimum age for solids. Some even suggest that the later you wean the better. However, both the WHO and the DoH agree that at about six months babies need more than just milk. Most can't feed themselves efficiently at this stage, so puréed food seems appropriate. Research has shown that 6% of babies still aren't reaching out for food at eight months, well beyond the age when they need it.

> 66 *I can see the point of baby-led weaning in terms of encouraging independence and letting the baby take their own time, but Satomi is not a good eater and I don't think she'd get enough nutrition. How can you expect a six-month-old baby to feed themselves enough?* 99
> **Kumiko, mum to Satomi, 8 months**

It's easier to provide a healthy balanced diet

When you give a baby puréed food, you have more control over what they're eating. Many mums find this reassuring when so much about bringing up a baby feels new and slightly daunting. You can prepare meals in advance or buy food in jars, pots or pouches and know what you're giving your baby.

If babies only eat puréed food, it is easier to give them a balanced diet that is low in salt and includes iron-rich foods, such as meat and fish. Of course, babies can still choose to eat or leave what is in the bowl. But if they are offered only appropriate purées, and not the other foods they see being eaten in the house, such as a bit of their dad's bacon or older brother's cake, it is easier.

You can hide food she doesn't like

If you find your baby doesn't really like a certain food, say meat or broccoli, then you can hide it in puréed dishes that your baby does like. For example, meat can be puréed and eaten with pasta, or broccoli can be added to shepherd's pie. Similarly, if a baby refuses to have milk, you can mix it with mashed potato, give it with Weetabix, or provide other dairy foods, such as yogurt, instead. If you were following BLW and serving only 'real' foods that your baby could eat with her hands, this may not be possible.

It's more convenient

Another advantage to purées, mentioned by many parents, is convenience (though fans of BLW might claim their method wins on that score). When your baby is ready to eat, even if you've just walked through the door, it doesn't take long to heat up a puréed meal from the freezer or open a jar. Likewise, if you're on holiday or out for the day, you can take a jar with you and it doesn't need to be kept cold. It can be more difficult to pack nutritious finger foods. Equally, if you go out unprepared, you can buy a jar quite easily almost anywhere. It may not be quite so straightforward to find something for your baby to feed herself that is suitable and not too salty.

Purées also make it easier to find a suitable place for your baby to have her meal. If you're on a family day trip, an eight-month-old baby can be fed a jar of pasta in her pushchair. For the BLWers, letting her loose on a similar hand-held meal in the buggy is likely to be problematic to say the least.

The disadvantages of purées

Making purées can be a chore

There's no denying it – cooking, puréeing and freezing baby meals is time consuming. You have to factor in not only the cooking time but also the time it takes to clear up, wash everything and portion the food out into ice-cube trays or little pots. Some of the recipes in the popular weaning books require as many as four pans plus a casserole dish! That's before you start thinking about chopping boards, moulis and ice-cube trays.

There isn't really a need to make complicated dishes for babies, but the instructions for some recipes require you to make your own stock before you even get started – which seems a lot of effort. Others have you skinning peaches or straining raspberries through muslin to remove the seeds.

TIP You may have heard stories of working mums getting up at 5am to make butternut squash risotto for their baby before they set off for work! When some parents find out that others are cooking everything from scratch, they find it hard to resist the pressure to do the same. If you enjoy cooking for your baby, that's great – but if you don't, then it can become an extra chore to try to fit into an already busy day.

66 *Overall I didn't find weaning fun. I steamed, mashed and froze ice cubes of loads of veg at a time – I found it annoying, messy, frustrating and never ending! Oh the joy when they can eat what you eat. I loved giving them finger food (cheese on toast, etc.) that they could just chew on for hours. Neither of mine were particularly fussy, so that helped, but I still found it such a chore.* 99
Vanessa, mum to Ellie, 3 years and Ruthie, 1 year

> ### Don't go overboard
> Peeling grapes, sieving kiwi fruit and making sandwiches that look like sailing boats really isn't necessary. Making purées and feeding your baby is pretty hands-on as it is, without being told you have to go the extra mile. There is no real reason to prepare food like this and it may even be counterproductive. Babies need to get used to different textures, and should learn to enjoy food for what it is, rather than being encouraged to eat more through gimmicks.

Some weaning recipes aren't very healthy

While purées can make it easier to give a nutritionally balanced diet, they don't make it a certainty. Some weaning recipes contain too many of the foods that previous generations thought of as good for 'building you up', including some meat and dairy products, which we now know are not so good for us. Ingredients like bacon and ham are best avoided because they contain too much salt. Processed meat products are also now believed by the World Cancer Research Fund (WCRF) to increase the risk of bowel cancer.

Other recipes contain large amounts of butter, cream and cheese. While babies do need a higher-fat diet than adults, it's better if they don't have too much saturated fat, which is found in meat and dairy foods. Babies, like the rest of us, should get their fat from a range of different foods, including oily fish and vegetable oils such as olive oil and rapeseed oil.

The recipes we've included in this book are simple, balanced and will be good for your baby.

Worries about what's being eaten

While knowing what your baby is eating makes planning a balanced diet easier, it can also lead to stress. When you make meals yourself, you know exactly what you've given your baby, but you can also see what's left in the bowl. It can be hard not to worry when your baby doesn't eat all the nutritious food you're providing. You may well worry that she isn't getting enough protein or isn't eating enough of anything. Such worries are usually completely unnecessary but that doesn't stop us worrying!

Feeling you have to use jars

The alternative to making baby meals yourself is to buy them, but this can be quite expensive and doesn't teach babies to enjoy homemade food. The pros and cons of commercially prepared baby food, compared with food you make yourself, are given on p86.

Be wary of who you listen to...

When reading weaning advice online, it's always worth taking a few moments to consider who is providing that advice. If it's someone who sells baby food, don't be surprised if they say babies need a lunch and dinner that are both 'proper' meals, for example beef casserole at midday then cod in cheese sauce for tea. Most adults don't eat like this; we're more likely to have something simpler at lunchtime. But when it comes to purées, this seems to be the general advice. For some parents, the only way to give their baby two meals like this every day is to resort to commercially prepared baby food (so the advice leads to more sales of their product). In Chapter 4 we'll show you there's more than one way to make sure your baby's nutritional needs are met, and that babies don't need two 'proper' meals every single day.

Problems moving on to lumps

When babies start with a completely puréed diet, there can sometimes be a problem getting them to move on to food with lumps. Recent research found it was best to introduce babies to lumpy food between six and nine months of age. Babies who weren't given lumps until later were found to be less likely to eat family meals at the age of 15 months, and to be seen by their mothers as fussy eaters and difficult to feed. It seems there is a window of opportunity when babies are open to trying different textures and eating lumpy food. If their meals are puréed for too long this can be missed, resulting in feeding problems. So, if you're going to start with purées, be careful not to miss this window.

66 *In my experience, eight months is the best time to get babies moving on from purées to lumpy food. I've seen a good few people who've left it too late and had problems. I knew an 18-month-old boy who would only eat purées*

from pouches. If you cook your own food it's easier, because you can do it gradually. But with jars it's more difficult. 🙶
**Jenny, mum of four, grandma of five, child-minder
for 'donkey's years' and currently nanny for Natasha,
19 months**

Problems getting used to real foods

Another related problem can be that, if they eat only mixed meals (such as pasta bolognaise, fish pie or chicken casserole), babies don't get used to the flavour and texture of individual foods. They may eat foods such as salmon or broccoli mixed with something else, but they aren't used to tasting them on their own, and they may not accept the foods when they are served this way when they're older.

Risks of overfeeding and weight problems

Most of us know that obesity is a growing problem among school children but we don't consider it an issue for babies. Chubby babies are viewed with affection and even pride. However, various studies have compared people's body weight when they were babies with weight in later life to see if chubby babies are more likely to become obese when they are older.

A review in the *British Medical Journal* found 11 different studies showing a connection – babies who were heavier, or particularly heavy compared to their height, were more likely to develop obesity in childhood, adolescence and adulthood. So while babies certainly shouldn't go on a diet, you mustn't encourage them to eat as much as they possibly can. Putting on weight rapidly and crossing from one centile line on the growth charts to the next isn't considered healthy.

What has this got to do with purées, you may ask? Well, babies who are spoon-fed are more likely to overeat than babies who feed themselves. This doesn't mean all spoon-fed babies are overfed. Often a baby will simply refuse to open her mouth for another spoonful or spit it out if she's had enough. But it's something parents should be aware of.

🙶 *I made porridge and purées, but it was baby-led in so far as I followed what they wanted. They liked most foods, but*

I never worried if they didn't finish. At the beginning of the meal, they'd be opening their mouths wide and obviously want feeding, but you could see when they weren't so keen. When they lost interest they'd stop opening their mouths so eagerly and they might start looking around at other things. **99**
Alice, mum to Lily, 4 years and Dylan, 2 years

With BLW, the problem of overfeeding isn't likely to occur, as babies feed themselves and can stop when they want. But with purées it can be an issue, so it's important for parents to listen when their baby says she's had enough. If a baby turns her head away, stops swallowing or gives other signs that she doesn't want to eat, then it's time to stop feeding. It can be hard if you've spent ages lovingly preparing a meal or if you're worried she doesn't eat enough, but food battles really are best avoided at this stage.

Babies don't learn independence

Another related problem is that sometimes parents continue to spoon-feed an older baby or toddler who is capable of feeding herself. It's important for babies to feed themselves when they become old enough, otherwise they may continue to eat just because food is being put into their mouths, even if they've had enough. This particularly affects babies who are easy going. Feeding with purées can be very quick, so a baby may eat a whole dish before their body has time to register when they are full.

You can't enjoy your own meal at the same time

The last problem related to feeding a baby with spoonfuls of purée concerns you more than your baby. Ideally your little one should be joining in family meals and eating at the same time as you and anyone else at home. This provides many advantages for your baby, which are discussed in more detail later (see p57). Babies who see other people eating tend to eat much better themselves, so shared meal times are ideal to encourage good eating habits. However, if you are using one hand to feed your baby, and are trying to keep track of how they are doing, it can be quite difficult to enjoy your own meal.

Pros and cons of purées in a nutshell

Pros
- You can feed a baby who doesn't have the skills to feed herself
- You can plan a balanced diet more easily
- You know what and how much has been eaten
- You can hide unpopular foods
- You can use jars of baby food if it is more convenient

Cons
- Preparing and freezing food take time
- Some babies refuse to eat lumps
- You get stressed when they don't eat the healthy food you've prepared
- Babies are sometimes overfed
- Moving to family meals can be difficult

It's now up to you to weigh up these pros and cons, and be aware of how to avoid some of the problems of using purées if this is the route you want to go down.

Parents' top tips for traditional weaning

- Do a purée swap. If you make a batch of a particular recipe and a friend does another, you can swap frozen meals. Then your baby can try different foods, and if they don't like it you won't end up with a freezer full of unwanted baby food.
- Try putting cheese sauce on foods your baby doesn't like. It hides the taste and they love it.
- Don't be scared to move your baby on from purées to normal foods. Given the chance, they can do it much quicker than you think.
- Invent your own baby foods – it's more fun than following recipes.

- If you have a garlic press at the dinner table you can quickly make baby food from whatever you're eating.
- When you're going out and taking food you prepared earlier, make it really dry. Then when you're out, you can just mix in some boiling water. This makes it runnier and warms it up at the same time.

3

Baby-led weaning

Baby-led weaning (BLW) involves letting your baby feed herself right from the start. Parents who take the BLW approach don't make purées and don't feed their baby with a spoon. Instead, your baby has only finger foods – and not just toast fingers or other hand-held snacks, but meat and two veg too.

If you haven't heard much about BLW before, you might be horrified by the thought of the likely mess or concerned that a baby wouldn't manage to eat enough. But the approach is rapidly gaining popularity, and growing numbers of parents are loudly singing its praises. Others think it sounds great in theory but find it doesn't always work in practice.

The term 'baby-led weaning' was brought to public attention in the UK by health visitor Gill Rapley in 2006. Since then it's been discussed in NCT publications, the national press and parenting magazines and on the popular parenting websites.

Most people assume BLW is a relatively new way of weaning, but this isn't really the case. Although it seemed like a new phenomenon in the media, mums have actually been feeding their babies in this way for years.

One of the main reasons BLW has taken off now is the change in advice from health professionals to wean at six months instead of four. When the majority of people were weaning their babies earlier,

BLW wasn't really feasible. Most four-month-old babies are not able to manage anything other than puréed food, but at six months babies can begin to handle food. Advocates say it fits in rather well with the current weaning recommendation, but later we'll consider more closely whether this really is the case. The DoH suggests parents start the weaning process with mashed foods at about six months and recommends the introduction of finger foods *when you feel your baby is ready* – and that's the key.

> 66 *I heard about BLW from a friend and tried it with Max. It was a bit of a leap of faith, but the theory made sense to me and it turned out to be so much easier. It's messy but it's worth it and it's only for a small amount of time – Max doesn't even need a bib now. I think it teaches babies to gag effectively and the only worrying choking incident I ever had was with Dexter. I would totally recommend it.* 99
> **Connie, mum to Dexter, 4 years and Max, 14 months**

The main features of BLW

- No spoon-feeding
- No purées or mashed meals
- Joining in family meals
- Babies choose what and how much to eat
- Never put food into a baby's mouth
- No coaxing to eat up

The theory behind BLW

The idea behind BLW is that babies don't need to be spoon-fed with puréed food. If you wait until they are naturally ready to be weaned, at about six months, then you can bypass purées and offer a selection of nutritious finger foods. This way they can feed themselves right from the beginning and start developing a healthy relationship with food.

The basis of the approach is really that babies should be free to explore and experiment with food when they're ready, without the help or interference of an adult. It is thought that this will help them learn to enjoy a varied diet right from the start.

Parents who've tried BLW believe it stops babies becoming fussy eaters and is less stressful than trying to 'force a baby to finish a jar of purée'. An important aspect of BLW is the emphasis on your baby being in control. Your baby goes at her own pace, and she eats whatever she wants and as much as she wants. She should join in family meals and be offered a selection of foods to choose from. BLW advocates say that parents are surprised at what a well-balanced diet babies choose when they are left to make their own decision.

The idea that babies can select a healthy diet for themselves isn't a new one. Clara Davis carried out a famous experiment in an orphanage in the 1930s in which 15 babies were allowed to self-select their diets. Everything the babies ate, from the very first mouthful, was carefully recorded. The babies stayed in the experiment for up to four and a half years and during this time their health was carefully monitored, including blood tests and X-rays, and they all appeared very healthy. Interestingly, she found that when babies were able to eat whatever they wanted from a range of healthy foods, they chose very different diets, but ones that were all nutritionally balanced in the long term.

This study is sometimes cited as proof that babies who are allowed to eat what they want will choose well and be healthy. But there is a very important difference between those children from the orphanage and babies of today: the range of foods available to them. Clara Davis's orphans chose from 33 foodstuffs (e.g. apples, tomatoes, chicken, haddock, oatmeal), none of them processed. They weren't even offered bread, fruit-flavoured yogurts or breakfast cereals, never mind the biscuits and sausages available in most modern households.

We can learn a lot from the experiment about letting babies have more control over what they eat, and we'll look at this more closely later (see p74), but this experiment did *not* involve BLW. Apart from the differences in foods available, the babies in the experiment were fed with spoons if they indicated to a nurse that they wanted to be, whereas spoon-feeding is against the strict BLW principles.

66 *Alexander was weaned in the normal way, but then we had friends doing baby-led weaning and we started doing it with Lucy. I thought it sounded like a great idea but she didn't really like it. She much preferred being fed. She's not that into food so she usually needs lots of distraction so that you can get some food into her.* 99
David, dad to Alexander, 2 years and Lucy, 12 months

Is it as good as you think?

There are many claims about the advantages of BLW that go beyond the realms of food and nutrition. It is said to be better for hand–eye co-ordination, the development of speech and for manual dexterity. And it seems logical that picking up food, getting it to your mouth and chewing can help with these skills. However, babies who start on purées can have finger foods as well. They can also play with toys and keys and wet wipes and other things babies seem to love. In fact, there are many activities that can help with a child's development. There is no evidence that babies who are weaned the BLW way are developmentally any more advanced than babies who start being weaned onto purées.

Those who promote BLW say it reduces the risk of a baby choking. This is often a fear when parents first think about giving their baby whole foods, such as broccoli florets or pieces of chicken. The theory is that when babies feed themselves, as they do with BLW, they take in the food at the front of their mouths and can move it to the back themselves, in a controlled way. When a baby slurps food off a spoon, it goes straight to the back of the mouth, where it presents a choking hazard. This may be why some babies who have got used to having very smooth purées, which can be slurped down like a smoothie or thick shake, find it hard to move on to lumpy foods, which need to be chewed before they are swallowed. Again, as with the claims that BLW is better for your baby's development, there is no evidence that babies are less likely to choke if you choose BLW. Likewise, there is nothing to suggest they are *more* likely to choke. If a baby is sitting up and feeding herself she may gag, but most learn very quickly to chew or gum food before trying to swallow it.

The controversy

As you can see from the two examples above, this isn't for everyone. Search the internet for information on BLW and you'll come across some very lively and heavy discussions. Its strongest advocates are staunch in their views, and unyielding in sticking to its principles; its fiercest critics accuse BLW of being a cult, while defenders say it is simply an ethos.

Either way, there are strong views about what parents should and shouldn't do if they want to call themselves BLWers. The most hotly debated topic is whether spoon-feeding or 'spoon-loading' is acceptable. If you're wondering what spoon-loading is, it's when you fill the spoon then give it to your baby to put into her own mouth.

Some mothers who have bottle-fed their babies have been made to feel slightly left out, as there is an emphasis on BLW being a natural progression from breastfeeding. In reality, there is no reason why bottle-fed babies should be weaned in a different way to those who are breastfed, but much of the online chat about BLW assumes babies are being breastfed. Breastfed babies appear to be better able to regulate their intake of milk according to their needs, so having control over their intake of solids is considered an extension of this.

TIP Regardless of the 'rules' of BLW, and the guilt that may accompany breaking these rules, BLW has a lot of good features. As parents, we need to take the positives and not the stress and guilt that can sometimes accompany this approach.

How to do BLW

Babies are usually at least six months old when they begin BLW. It is important that they are able to sit up and grasp objects by themselves. You can either sit your baby on your lap when you're eating as a family, or put her in a highchair or Bumbo and give her some food so she can join in.

To start with, your baby may just play with the food or perhaps suck on it but not actually eat it. For some babies it's a while before they're really eating much food, but others appear to get the hang of things more quickly.

The traditional weaning advice is to start with one meal a day, and then progress to two and then three daily meals. However, with BLW, it is advised that from six months you should give your baby some food every time *you* eat. The aim is to give her plenty of opportunities to learn about food and how to feed herself.

For the first few months, meal times should be viewed as 'playtime' and you should give meals when your baby isn't hungry. The theory is that if your baby is hungry she will get frustrated. The BLW guidelines are quite clear that even if your baby seems hungry and frustrated, you shouldn't help her to get the food to her mouth. A baby of six to about nine months is, according to BLW advocates, hungry for milk but not for solids, and doesn't actually need solids for the first few months of weaning. We'll go back to this (see p64) if that sounds strange to you!

> TIP Remember babies can't eat everything you do. Revisit our list of what to feed your baby when (see p23). If you're going to try BLW, keep the list in mind.

Babies should be offered a selection of nutritious finger foods to choose from. As most six-month-old babies aren't good at picking up small objects, it's not a good idea to cut up food into very small pieces. Later, when you can see that your baby has a reasonable pincer grip and can pick up objects between her thumb and forefinger, you can give smaller pieces of food.

If you are going to do BLW, start with foods that are easy to grasp and not too slippery, such as cooked broccoli, which has a natural 'handle', or hand-sized pieces of other vegetables or fruit. Food such as carrot or cucumber can be cut into fat chip shapes about 5cm long. Then, when your baby picks one up in her fist, it will stick out the end and she'll be able to get at it. Vegetables will need to be cooked till they're soft, so that your baby can chew them easily – imagine trying to eat a raw carrot with no teeth!

> TIP Place food straight on the highchair tray or the table, rather than in a bowl or on a plate.

It's best to give one or two pieces of food at a time rather than everything at once. If a baby has more than that it can be overwhelming, and there's more chance of it ending up on the floor.

Good foods to start with

- Whole cooked vegetables, such as green beans and baby corn
- Cooked broccoli florets
- Vegetable sticks, including carrot, potato and pumpkin
- Chicken and meat strips
- Toast fingers
- Breadsticks
- Strips of raw cucumber and peppers
- Sticks of hard cheese

Remember: The DoH recommends the introduction of some of these foods only after six months of age.

You'll notice a big difference in the guidelines for BLW compared with the traditional weaning approach outlined in the last chapter. With purées, there is a series of stages that your baby moves through according to her age. With BLW, however, because you begin after six months, the range of foods you offer is much wider right from the start. Once babies have got used to eating some solids, it's suggested that you then give them more variety and a wider range of textures. The idea is to be guided by your baby and let her try anything she wants. However, some parents wait a while before introducing foods such as curries.

Foods to move on to

- Spicy food
- Dips such as houmous
- Thick soups such as lentil and vegetable
- Raw vegetables

The advantages of BLW

There are many advantages to BLW, and although its fans have put forward some doubtful claims, this shouldn't distract from the great features it does offer.

Eating together is better for everyone

The emphasis on family meals and giving a baby control over the weaning process is a really positive thing. Academics and health professionals both agree that family meals are extremely important and encourage healthy eating habits. Babies love to join in, and if they see other people eating healthy food, and enjoying it, they are likely to follow suit.

Even if ultimately you do not end up following the BLW approach, sharing family meals from as early an age as possible is an aspect that can benefit all babies. Children who eat with adults are likely to be less fussy about their food and to eat more healthily.

Babies get used to family meals

BLW can also avoid one of the potential pitfalls of purées: that babies given specially prepared meals don't get used to ordinary family meals. Parents often follow weaning recipes they'd be unlikely to choose for themselves. If you are not keen on eating chicken with apricots, or fish in cheese sauce, then why make it for your baby? Similarly, do you really want your baby to get a taste for dishes such as broccoli with pears?

By the end of weaning, you want your baby to join in with healthy family meals. So it's better to get babies used to eating the kind of dishes they'll have when they're older. This is what happens with BLW, as ideally your baby eats what the rest of the family is having. Some foods, such as a spicy curry, aren't appropriate at the beginning, but if you are doing BLW, your little one is encouraged to share in the majority of meals.

You can enjoy your meal at the same time

Since you don't need to spoon-feed your baby, you are free to enjoy your own meal at the same time. This is a significant benefit that most people don't really appreciate until they've sat down to eat with their baby and have found they end up with a plate of cold food for themselves.

Also, if your baby eats first, she may well demand to get down and play or want to be carried when it's your turn to eat. Parents of young children often complain about having to bolt down their meals because there never seems to be enough time to eat. Having the same food as your baby, at the same time, may not appear to be a particularly sophisticated dining experience, as they mush potato into their hair, but in some ways it's a more civilised way of eating. You can chat and enjoy the food together.

It's fun!

BLW can be really fun – for the baby and the parents. BLW advocates love watching their babies tackle all kinds of food, and sometimes in quite unexpected ways. Eating should be a pleasurable part of life and it's lovely to see a baby giving things a go and enjoying food.

> 66 *BLW just seems completely natural to me and I loved doing it with Florence. From six months old she would grab at ingredients to eat when I was cooking – carrots, mushroom, broccoli. Before long she had tried a plethora of food when she wanted to. I was brought up eating the same food as my parents and now she eats the same as us. There's nothing she won't eat.* 99
> *Nancy, mum to Florence, 23 months*

Less fussy eating means less stress for you

Parents who have used BLW often say they think it helped prevent their little one becoming a fussy eater. Although no formal research has been carried out comparing fussy eating among those weaned via BLW or purées, it is a theme that comes up repeatedly.

This may be partly that parents have different expectations. If, during Sunday lunch, you give your child a bit of everything and find she eats stuffing, roast potatoes, carrots and cauliflower, but leaves the chicken, you may think 'great, she's not fussy'. Or perhaps you've just been giving her bits of food throughout the meal and haven't really noticed what she's eaten. However, if you have spent all morning following a weaning recipe for chicken casserole, including making your own stock, only to find your little angel won't eat it, you're likely to have a less relaxed view. The baby in the first case will probably be given chicken again and may grow to like it, but the mother who made the special meal could decide her baby is fussy and doesn't like chicken.

Giving a baby lots of opportunities to try different foods, without any pressure to eat them, is the best way to encourage her to be an adventurous eater. A baby may just want to look at something the first time they are given it. Then they may choose to squish it, lick it or just push it around before eating it. BLW encourages this kind of experimentation. It doesn't mean that parents who follow the traditional approach can't give their babies the same opportunities, but, with BLW, playing with food is an explicit part of the weaning process.

No purées to make

Another advantage to BLW is that you don't have to spend hours puréeing vegetables, nor do you have to buy baby food, as the whole family eats the same food. If you've made purées for a baby in the past or talked to friends about it, you'll know how time consuming it can be. Most people who make purées for their baby make batches and freeze them. In theory this saves time as you don't have to make fresh meals every day. However, babies tend to have two proper cooked meals a day, which means 14 meals a week, so you end up having to cook more often than you might like. And if you spend time making special meals only to find they're rejected, it can be frustrating. If you're just giving your baby a bit of your own dinner, you'll probably be less anxious about it being eaten.

> 66 BLW worked really well for us and gave us a great option for introducing food in an enjoyable way for Elsie. It means she's always been a very independent eater and has never had any objection to textures or lumpy food. She has pretty limited tastes though – fruit never seemed to be a preference and from about 11 months she decided she wasn't keen on vegetables, so we struggle with her fruit and veg intake now. 99
> **Melissa, mum to Elsie, 16 months**

Overfeeding is less likely

Because your baby is feeding herself, she can stop when she's had enough, which can be a problem with spoon-feeding (see p67). Some advocates of BLW say this issue is contributing to the increasing rates of obesity. But let's keep things in perspective – spoon-feeding is not the same as force-feeding, as some BLWers might imply.

It's also worth remembering that babies have been spoon-fed with mushed food for generations, but it is only relatively recently that we have seen rapidly escalating levels of childhood obesity. It's naïve to think that BLW might be the answer to the nation's obesity problem. However, overfeeding and ignoring signs of fullness obviously aren't a good idea at any age, and babies should be able to stop eating when they want.

The disadvantages of BLW

It's messy!

There's no denying it: BLW is messy. Very, very messy. And food gets wasted. This can make eating out more difficult, as you don't want to give your baby food that has been dropped on the floor of a café. Nor do you want to cover a friend's floor with half-chewed vegetables! See p13 for some de-mess devices.

Meals take a long time

Meals can take longer, particularly at the start, when food is often dropped or squished. We've discussed the benefits of this: if you're eating at the same time it allows you to do so at your own pace. But if you're not eating or you want to go out or get on with other things, then long meals can be a disadvantage.

Parents worry about choking

When people first hear about BLW, they are often concerned about the risk of choking. Although there is no evidence that the risk is any higher with BLW than with purées, it's still a real fear for parents.

There are 15,000 cases of choking reported to hospitals each year among the under-fives. About half of these are incidents involving food, and it's important to recognise that babies and toddlers can't always cope with the same foods that adults eat. They don't have as many teeth and they're still getting used to chewing and swallowing, and co-ordinating these activities with breathing. The most common causes of choking in under-fives are sweets and fish bones, but meat products such as sausages and burgers can also cause problems, as can vegetables and whole nuts. It can be fun giving babies the opportunity to get used to normal adult foods, but it's important to remember that they're not little adults and it needs to be done carefully. This is important however you start weaning.

> 66 I started giving Ben purées when he was six months old but he just wasn't interested. After trying for a month or so, my health visitor suggested giving him finger foods instead. I didn't use any books but I suppose it was baby-led weaning. I just gave him what we were eating and it seemed to work. I didn't have the same problem with Celina so she was weaned with purées. They both eat pretty much anything and everything now. 99
> **Helena, mum to Ben, 2 and Celina, 16 months**

TIP Choking or gagging is also an issue with traditional weaning (see p53). Unfortunately, the risk of choking exists whatever method you choose. See p32 for ways to minimise this risk.

It's harder to plan a balanced diet

A big concern with BLW is whether a baby's diet is always appropriate nutritionally. One side of this is whether a baby will miss out on certain foods and therefore nutrients. This is mainly a problem in the first few months. The other is whether they will eat inappropriate foods, particularly those that are too high in salt.

Babies can miss out on essential nutrients

There are a number of ways in which babies doing BLW can miss out. If a baby is only eating what she can pick up and get to her mouth, she can't eat foods she's unable to grasp and feed to herself. Research has shown that when babies reach six months, half of them aren't yet reaching out for food. So, to go from this to feeding yourself full meals is quite a journey and some babies won't eat anything much for quite a while.

Even those who are reaching out for foods may struggle at the beginning. They may miss out on things like meat and fish, because small pieces can't be grasped and larger pieces are difficult to chew. Some babies are fine with these foods right from the beginning and will happily gum bits of meat or chew on a chicken leg. But if not, babies can miss out on iron and omega 3 fatty acids.

They may also be hampered by other difficulties of feeding themselves. Take, for example, a nutritionally balanced meal, such as spaghetti bolognaise with a sauce that contains beef, tomatoes and carrots. It's not hard to picture the result: most of the sauce falls off the spaghetti and ends up on the tray, the floor or their face and hands. This means that what your baby actually eats is mainly carbohydrate, without the protein and nutrients that the meat and vegetables supply.

Excluding foods to reduce the mess?

BLW fans are keen to explain how babies can eat yogurt by putting their face in the pot, or enjoy a bowl of porridge with their hands. In practice, parents keen to reduce the mess sometimes avoid giving these foods to their baby, which means she misses out on the nutrients they contain. Otherwise, they go against the BLW 'ethos' and feed porridge or other runny foods to their baby with a spoon. This is probably a better approach and we explore this more balanced view in the next chapter.

The idea that a baby will choose a nutritionally balanced diet is a great one in theory. In practice, it depends not only on your baby being capable of eating whatever she wants, but also on there being a wide range of foods available daily. Nobody is going to cook and lay out a large selection of foods three times a day. This means that babies can't really choose anything they want. They can only decide to take or leave the limited number of foods on offer at each meal. In itself this isn't bad, as your baby needs to get used to eating what's on offer, rather than being fussy. But it means a baby may not be in a position to choose a healthy balanced diet for herself.

> 66 I tried BLW with Elliot and it was great. I was a bit worried he would choke but he had a good (if slightly alarming) technique for expelling anything he couldn't swallow. The downside to BLW is that, eating more 'grown-up' foods, he probably had a bit more salt than he should. Also, he still puts pretty much anything in his mouth so I regularly have to pluck out small toys, buttons, etc. that he's decided to sample. 99
> Adrienne, mum to Calvin, 4 years and Elliot, 2 years

Delayed weaning may cause problems

With BLW, solids are likely to be introduced after six months; indeed, advocates of BLW say it's fine for babies to start weaning whenever you think they're ready, even if that's seven, eight or nine months old, or even later. However, this isn't supported by any evidence and may be a cause for concern. There is now speculation that introducing a baby to certain foods later than six months could increase the risk of dietary problems. This is part of the reason why the European Food Standards Agency recommend that weaning should take place between four and six months.

Lessons from Sweden

In Sweden, parents used to be advised to introduce gluten, which is found in wheat, at four months. Then, in 1982, the official advice changed to six months. It was then found that the rate of coeliac disease (gluten intolerance) increased. They thought that this increase suggested that babies needed to have gluten earlier, in order for their bodies to get used to it. So, in 1996, the Swedish authorities decided to change the advice back and recommended weaning from four months again. They also advised parents to introduce gluten slowly while breastfeeding. Interestingly, the country then saw a sharp decline in the incidence of coeliac disease, back to previous levels.

This example alone doesn't mean that babies in the UK should immediately start having gluten from four months. The findings could be just a coincidence, or something else may have been going on at the same time that was responsible for the changing rates of coeliac disease. But it does raise the question about whether, when it comes to weaning, we should be thinking 'the later the better'. Introducing higher-risk foods later may increase the risk of an allergy or intolerance, rather than reduce it. There is more about this in Chapter 11 on allergies (see p196).

Research has shown that eight-month-old babies who have a lot of milk, rather than solids, are more likely to be anaemic. Some health experts argue that weaning should begin before six months because by then the nutrient stores a baby is born with are running out. Therefore the idea that it's fine for a baby to just play with food and hardly eat anything at all until nine or so months should be viewed with caution.

Relying on milk to supply everything

With BLW, babies don't usually eat much at first, and according to BLWers this doesn't matter. The argument is that babies are getting all the calories and nutrients they need from breast milk so they don't really need food until they're at least eight or nine months old. The first few months of weaning are considered a time for experimenting with food and for your baby to learn how to feed herself. Parents are therefore encouraged not to worry about how much is being eaten.

This is wrong. Although learning about food and self-feeding are vital aspects of development, a baby also needs nutrients. At around six months, babies need foods other than milk to supply the iron and other nutrients they require. This is why the DoH recommends solids at six months. Research has shown that one in five babies are anaemic at eight months of age, and babies who have more than six breastfeeds per day, or more than 600ml of formula, are particularly at risk. This is because they are having less iron-rich food, such as meat and fortified breakfast cereals. Breast milk or formula is not a substitute for solids once a baby gets to about six months. The evidence shows that babies need both. So while it is important for babies to have some control over their feeding, it is also worth considering whether some babies are missing out on nutrients simply because they aren't capable of feeding themselves very well.

> 66 *A friend told me about baby-led weaning and I started by giving Myla anything I would have puréed. She had chunks of roasted root vegetables and I might make soup and scoop out the lumpy bits and give them to her. I followed all the official rules with my son but not with Myla – she's happy eating sandwiches and crisps now, and she loves biscuits.* 99
> **Genevieve, mum to Callum, 8 years and Myla, 18 months**

Eating foods with too much salt and sugar

With BLW, babies may end up eating inappropriate foods, particularly foods with a high salt content. Foods available in restaurants and cafés tend to be particularly salty, so although it may be easy to find something on the menu your baby will happily eat (the convenient side to BLW), the food may not be nutritionally suitable. Products such as chips often come already salted, even if you get a children's meal. Foods that you might think of as healthier, such as roast potatoes and boiled vegetables, may not be much better, as they too will usually have been cooked with salt.

If you eat out only very occasionally, say once a month, or if your baby is just having a taste of these foods, it's not a huge problem. In fact, trying new foods is always to be encouraged. But if you and your baby regularly eat at cafés or restaurants, then you can see how important it is to choose foods carefully. The alternative is to take a lunch box for your baby, but this goes against the convenience of your baby eating the same food as adults.

Salty foods to be aware of
- Ham and bacon
- Smoked salmon
- Salami
- Pepperoni pizza
- Salted chips (e.g. fast food)
- Tapas (e.g. chorizo, Spanish omelette)

The real advantages are sometimes lost

Another problem found by some parents is that their baby's meal times don't fit in with their own. For example, Dad doesn't get home from work until after 7pm, but the baby needs to go to bed at 7.30. This means that one of the most important aspects of BLW, the baby joining in with family meals, doesn't work. Even if a parent is able to eat at the same time as the baby, they may still end up having different things. This is most likely to happen at lunchtime, when many adults have a sandwich, while babies who are just starting to wean need cooked, softer food.

Pros and cons of BLW in a nutshell

Pros
- The baby is in control at meal times
- No cooking special baby meals, puréeing or freezing
- Problems moving from purées to lumps are avoided
- Overfeeding is unlikely
- It encourages more adventurous eating and less fussiness
- The focus on family meals encourages healthier eating habits

Cons
- Adult foods can be too salty for babies
- Babies can only eat a food if they can feed it to themselves
- Babies may miss out on certain foods and therefore nutrients
- It's messy
- It's not suitable for all babies
- Parents feel guilty if they 'break the rules', e.g. by using spoon-feeding

---

Is BLW suitable for everyone?

Advocates of BLW acknowledge that it may not suit all babies. If you have a family history of allergies or food intolerances, you will have to be more careful about what you give your baby. You may not be able to let your baby choose from the range of foods you would like. It is also a good idea to introduce higher-risk foods individually, rather than letting your baby go at her own pace. But this doesn't mean you can't enjoy eating with your baby and letting her feed herself.

If your baby was born prematurely, some aspects of BLW may not be appropriate or it may be better to start with purées. Likewise, if your baby has special needs that affect her fine motor skills, this will affect her ability to pick up foods and feed herself, so it may be better to use a combination of purées and self-feeding.

Is BLW really stress-free?

The idea of BLW sounds lovely and easy and stress-free, but in practice some parents find they can't stick to the 'rules'. This is because most families don't sit down together three times a day for a nutritionally balanced meal. One or both parents may work long hours, which can mean family meals aren't practical. Some find they eat at a friend's house, so they decide to spoon-feed their baby on these occasions to avoid too much mess. Others feel their baby isn't that interested in food or isn't gaining weight as she should be, so they have to spoon-feed their baby to get enough food into her. It's then common for parents to feel as if they're 'failing', for not managing to live up to the BLW ideal, and not providing their baby with all the advantages that fans claim it provides.

Some parents feel they'd like to try BLW but it seems a bit 'cult-ish'. This is particularly true of mothers who bottle-fed their baby, as they feel BLW excludes them and focuses on breastfed babies. There is also quite a bit of talk on the BLW forums about how natural both breastfeeding and BLW are, and how they go together to give babies the best start in life. There's no evidence for this, but it can add to any guilt mothers might be feeling if they aren't breastfeeding, and some mums find this to be quite alienating.

The great spoon debate

There is heated debate among BLWers about the use of spoons. If you've looked at any BLW website you may well have seen it. Those who follow BLW strictly don't like to say spoon-feeding isn't 'allowed', but they say it isn't 'necessary'. In effect, this seems to mean the same thing – you shouldn't do it.

However, some parents find their baby just can't manage to eat certain foods, like soup or yogurt, without being spoon-fed. They argue that their baby obviously wants to eat certain things, but she can't manage to get spoonfuls to her mouth without spilling it all. When this is the case, and the baby shows signs that she is happy to be spoon-fed, should it really be considered such a taboo? BLW purists argue that as soon as you use a spoon the baby is no longer in control. Instead, you are, and therefore there's a risk of overfeeding. But spoon-feeding shouldn't be seen as force-feeding, and it seems slightly unkind to watch a baby get frustrated because the spoon is always empty by the time she gets it to her mouth.

Of course, it could be argued that spoon-feeding a baby who wants to be spoon-fed is being baby-led. Others would rather make soup with bigger bits in that their baby can eat more easily, or buy thicker yogurt. However, some would say this goes against the ethos of BLW being easy because babies join in with any family meal. Spoon-loading is seen as acceptable to all but the strictest BLWers, but the spoon can still end up empty by the time a baby gets it to her mouth. This leads on to the debate about how much 'help' you can give your baby in getting the spoon to her mouth.

And we go round in circles… This is another example of where we as parents need to use a large dose of our common sense. See Chapter 4 for a more balanced and practical approach to weaning, and spoons!

> 66 I did BLW with Lydia and it's been so much fun. My friend who's doing it was really strict about not using a spoon and got really stressed because her baby couldn't manage to eat much for a few months. He was really hungry and it affected his sleep. But I've just spoon-fed Lydia foods like Weetabix and bolognaise. Otherwise it would be so messy and she wouldn't be able to eat much even if she wanted to. 99
> **Stephanie, mum to Caleb, 2 years and Lydia, 14 months**

BLW is a very interesting idea, and for those unaware of any alternative to spoon-feeding it is a great eye-opener. The focus on family meals and giving babies more control over what and how much they eat is certainly beneficial. However, you may find that following what can be seen as the 'rules' is incredibly and unnecessarily stressful. Some just take what they want from the approach and leave the rest. Others see it as an all-or-nothing approach, and if they use a spoon some of the time they feel it's a backward step in their baby's progress.

TIP The debate around self-feeding can easily distract from the aim of weaning, which is essentially to provide a well-balanced diet and get your baby used to enjoying healthy meals. It's important for you to follow your instincts when trying to achieve these aims, and for some this means following a more flexible, less rigid approach.

Top tips from baby-led weaners

- Use a crinkle cutter for foods like mango to make them less slippery and easier to grip.
- Get an easy-to-clean highchair, ideally one that you can hose down or put in the shower.
- Pasta twists are better than spaghetti or tubes as the sauce doesn't come off them so easily.
- Bibs with sleeves save on washing clothes.
- When you're giving chicken, the leg meat is better than the breast. It's not so dry so it's easier to eat and less likely to cause choking.
- If your baby doesn't eat the foods you give her, you can always purée them or mash them up and offer them on a spoon – it's cheating but it means she can eat if she wants to.
- Mash up uneaten food and put it on toast; that way you're not giving an alternative, but making it easier for your baby to eat it if she wants to.

4

The balanced approach

Now we've looked at the two approaches in detail, let's take it one step further. This chapter describes a more balanced approach that takes the best bits of baby-led weaning (BLW) and traditional weaning and combines them. The general idea is described here, and then in Part two we'll go through each stage of weaning to see what you should be doing in practical terms. There isn't a strict set of rules and a timetable to follow, because it's important to recognise that babies are all different. Instead there is advice about what to do and how to progress, depending on how you and your baby are finding things.

The balanced approach involves keeping an open mind and realising there are many different, but equally good, ways to feed a baby. As most parents find sooner or later, you can follow all the plans from all the books you want, but unless your baby is on the same page, it probably won't work. So you need to be ready to adapt. You may decide to start weaning at six months, only to find your baby isn't at all keen on that idea. Alternatively, purées may suit you both for a while, and then one day your baby decides she wants to feed herself from now on, and any attempt by you to spoon-feed her will be resisted. If you can avoid having a rigid approach, it will save you a lot of stress.

> TIP It's vital for you to remember that your baby isn't doomed to a lifetime of fussy eating if you feed her with a spoon sometimes. And if you don't provide organic butternut squash or quinoa, it doesn't make you a bad parent!

While it's important to follow some basic guidelines, to keep your baby safe and provide the nutrients she needs, there's still plenty of scope for flexibility. The guidelines showing which food groups make up a balanced diet (see p105), as well as which foods to avoid (see p23), are based on scientific evidence. But suggestions from health visitors or books that you start with baby rice or florets of steamed broccoli are just that, personal suggestions. There isn't any evidence to suggest that feeding particular foods in a particular order will make any difference.

> 66 We know children who are very picky eaters and we didn't want food to be an issue with Archie. We encourage him to use his hands if he wants to and we never worry if he doesn't eat. He used to eat on his own, but as he got bigger it seemed wrong and now we all eat together at the weekend and whenever we can. If we have stew or casserole we'll make two pots so he has the same but with less spice and without the salt. 99
> Ray, dad to Archie, 2 years

Keeping meal times relaxed and enjoyable is just as important as the food your baby eats. Weaning a baby is about teaching her good habits and a healthy attitude to food as much as about providing nutrients. Taking a balanced approach means realising that both spoon-feeding and self-feeding can have a place in your baby's eating, especially at the beginning. You may find there are times when your baby refuses to be spoon-fed, so give her more finger foods. Likewise, if you've been giving her finger foods but she's underweight and not that interested, or if she's just tired, then spoon-feed her.

So what's best – purées or baby-led weaning?

Of course, there's no short answer to this one. We've looked at the advantages and disadvantages of both approaches – and there are quite a few of each! This debate can be very helpful because it makes you think about the importance of family meals and giving babies control over how much they want to eat. These factors are important whichever way you wean your baby.

It is also important to give your baby a variety of nutritious foods and to avoid certain foods whether you're giving them as purées *or* finger food. When you look at it this way, you can see there are lots of similarities between traditional weaning and BLW.

So the debate then comes down to whether to start with purées and spoon-feeding, or to give a baby pieces of food for self-feeding. In the early days, from about six to nine months, this can make quite a difference to the amount of food a baby actually eats. And while advocates of BLW might argue that babies only need milk at this stage, research suggests that this isn't the case. We know six-month-old babies need more nutrients than milk alone can provide. So, if your six-month-old can feed herself efficiently, then BLW is great; but if she can't, then purées are the obvious answer. But experimenting and learning how to handle real pieces of food are also beneficial at this stage, or as soon as you feel ready to start.

> 66 *We started baby-led weaning at five and a half months – well, we were more playing at the start. Then we officially started weaning at six months and went from purées to more lumpy food fairly quickly as she took to it well. We've tried to make eating fun and something to enjoy and it seems to have worked. I think you have to let your little one get messy and explore with their hands, and, most importantly, try and relax during meal times.* 99
> **Emma, mum to Alice, 11 months**

Finding a balance

It is possible to strike a balance between letting babies learn for themselves and ensuring they have the nutrients they need for healthy growth and development. By taking this balanced approach, you can ensure your baby gets the right nutrients and develops a healthy relationship with food, while alleviating your own stress and worries.

The great spoon debate (see p67) aside, there is plenty of evidence to show that other aspects of how you go about weaning, such as whether you eat together, provide a varied diet and respond to your baby's cues, can have a long-term impact. These factors can influence your baby's chances of becoming obese, developing iron deficiency and being a fussy eater. Below you'll find five features of weaning that are key to success. These have been drawn up using both evidence from scientific research and the experiences of real mums and dads – what they've found works and what they've struggled with. We will look at each one in turn to see what they mean at a practical level.

The key features

The five key features of the balanced approach are:

- trusting your baby
- family meals
- good nutrition
- experimenting
- flexibility.

By taking the best of both worlds, this approach could be described as BLW with some spoon-feeding at the beginning and greater flexibility; or traditional weaning with more finger foods and experimentation. Either way, it's not a radical new method, but something parents have been doing for years – and something that really works. Whether you have breastfed or bottle-fed your baby, you can take this balanced approach to weaning that will let your baby learn to enjoy a healthy and varied diet.

Start with trusting yourself

Don't forget how important your own common sense and parental instincts are. These are often overlooked, and when people are having their second or third child you'll often hear them say they wish they'd trusted their own instinct more with their first.

Instinct can't tell you the nutrients your baby needs or how much salt is in a product, but it can help you navigate the weaning process successfully. For example, if you open a jar of baby food that says it's nutritionally balanced and carefully designed for your baby's needs but you can't stand even the smell of it, well perhaps it's not the right thing to give her.

Likewise, if your health visitor is telling you that you must wait until six months to wean, but you really feel your five-month-old baby is ready, and you know the evidence shows it's OK, then use your common sense. Most mums find their health visitors invaluable, but some feel their advice can be a little too rigid at times. Even the official guidelines allow for individual differences.

> **❝** *I started Carter with BLW and it was great, but meals could take up to two hours by the time I'd finished cleaning everything! And the way he tackled yogurt was cute but not really effective. So I tweaked things and spoon-fed him things like yogurt and apple purée. And when he stopped eating broccoli I gave it mushed up with something else. I wanted him to get used to different textures and know that smooth foods are OK, just like chicken legs or crunchy carrots. He has a nice natural confidence with food now.* **❞**
> **Saskia, mum to Carter, 13 months**

1. Trust your baby

Something that comes up repeatedly in research is the importance of responding to a baby's cues about what they want to eat. We looked earlier at Clara Davis's experiment in the 1930s and there is a lot we can learn from it (see p52). The study had limitations, including the fact that it looked at only 15 children. Also there was no control group, so we don't know what would have happened if a similar group of babies had been put in an identical orphanage and fed set meals. Would they have eaten just as well and been as healthy as the babies who chose their own food? There's no way of knowing, but it does seem that if babies are allowed to eat what they want, from a healthy range of foods, they do surprisingly well, so we can afford to relax a little.

When a baby doesn't want to eat, there is often a valid reason. Sometimes you'll find out what that reason is but often you won't. Just as a baby's growth and development can seem to move on in fits and starts, so does her appetite and her interest in food. This is quite normal, although when you've carefully prepared something special for your baby, it can be rather frustrating.

Don't play games

It can be tempting to try to distract your baby and sneak in a few more mouthfuls, especially if she is underweight or you're worried she'll be hungry and won't sleep. Some parents end up playing elaborate games to get their baby to eat more than she really wants to. But try to resist. If a baby eats as much as she wants, it will help her stay in touch with her body's own cues for hunger and fullness. Trying to get babies to eat more food with distraction, or bribery and punishments when they're a bit older, can lead to food battles and other problems.

> 66 Whenever Nathanial is ill he goes off his food. Last year he was in intensive care twice, with suspected asthma. He lost a lot of weight and following this we saw a dietitian who recommended we offer one meal, with no alternatives if this was refused. We were advised this would also prevent fussy eating. I found it hard at first, as I was concerned his weight would plummet further, but over time it did work and his appetite improved. 99
> **Sarah, mum to Nathanial, 19 months**

TIP Don't be surprised if your baby has sudden changes in taste. Babies and toddlers sometimes love a food for weeks or even months, and then they won't touch it. It's something lots of parents notice and there is no real explanation for it. This can be frustrating, particularly if you thought you'd come up with a popular dish at last, but it's quite normal for babies to change their tastes.

Trust, but only so far

While it appears from the 1930s experiment that babies can eat healthily when they're in control, we have to remember that the babies involved didn't have access to the foods we have today. They were only ever offered unprocessed foods. We can't isolate our babies like this, so that they grow up never seeing processed foods, so it's a completely different ball game. Even if you kept bread, cereal and other processed foods out of sight at home, you'd have to boycott playgroups and friends' houses if you wanted to avoid biscuits. When faced with less healthy processed foods, we shouldn't assume babies know how much is good for them. It comes down to balance again – babies should have plenty of control over what they eat, but you have to be sensible about it.

Enough is enough

When you're feeding your baby, watch carefully for signs that she's had enough. These may include:

- spitting out food
- not opening her mouth for a spoon
- turning her head away
- crying
- keeping food in her mouth but not swallowing.

When you see these signs, or your baby shows you in other ways that she's had enough, it's time to end the meal.

A baby's weight gain is usually a fairly good indicator of how well she's growing. It is generally a good sign when her weight follows the growth curves in the charts, whether your little one is on the 98th centile or the 2nd. In the past, when it came to a baby's weight gain, people often took the view 'the more the better'. Chubby babies are still seen by many as bonny and thriving. However, a review of 24 studies published in the *British Medical Journal* showed that babies who put on weight more quickly are more likely to be obese when they grow up. A steady weight gain is best; we shouldn't get babies to eat as much as possible.[1]

2. Family meals

Several studies have found that the more often children eat with their family, the more likely they are to have a healthy diet.

Research shows that children who eat with their family at least three times a week are:

- 12% less likely to be overweight
- 20% less likely to eat junk food
- 24% more likely to eat fruit and vegetables
- 35% less likely to suffer from eating problems.

The reason why family meals are so great is that when children eat with others they talk more, eat more slowly and eat less. They are also likely to mimic the eating habits of the other people they're with, which should hopefully be a positive thing. Family meals have also been found to have a better nutrient content than those thrown together just for one person. It's good to enjoy the social element of meals, as well as seeing them as a time for refuelling. When we all lead such busy lives, they're a valuable time for just being together and enjoying each other's company. It's good to get into the habit of eating together, as family meals go on benefiting children right up to their teenage years.

It's best to cook family meals yourself whenever possible, and give a small portion to your baby. This way your baby will get used to eating what you eat. However, if you do this, don't add salt or sugar, at least not until you have taken out your baby's share. Check the labels on items such as stock, sauces, soups and ready meals as these can be particularly salty. If you want to eat foods like this yourself sometimes, then it might be better to give your baby something different. You can still eat together and there are probably some parts of the meal that everyone can have, but it's something that needs a bit of planning. For example, you could all have pasta, even if you have it with different sauces.

Eating with your baby can have positive effects on your own eating habits too. If you know you eat too many ready meals or processed foods such as sausages, then now is a good time to make some changes. It's also good if you eat a variety of different vegetables. It's great if you give your baby foods such as avocado, spinach and cauliflower, but if the only vegetable you eat is peas, there's a good chance she'll follow suit sooner or later. So if your diet needs improving, what better incentive is there to start making small changes, so that eventually you can all eat healthy meals together.

Even if your baby doesn't notice what you're eating now, and doesn't think she's missing out when you have chocolate or something else you'd rather she didn't eat, she soon will. If you don't eat certain healthy foods, such as fish or green vegetables, it's much harder to get your baby to eat them and enjoy them in the longer term. Even if she accepts them as a baby, research has shown repeatedly that children soon end up eating pretty much the same food as their parents.

66 *When each of them was a baby, I would usually feed them first, but as soon as you could put a bowl down in front of them and they could get on with it, they'd eat with everyone else. When we're at home, we'll always have breakfast and lunch together. My husband is usually home late, but I'll eat tea with them too most days. I've never been rigid about it – whatever works works.* 99
Deirdre, mum to Cormac, 7 years, Caoimhe, 6 years, Cliona, 4 years and Rowan, 3 years

If you feed your baby while you and any other family members eat, it can also make life easier, as you need to cook only one meal. Also, your baby will have the opportunity to experiment with food while you have time to enjoy your own meal.

3. Good nutrition

A baby's diet should provide her with all the nutrients she needs for healthy growth and development. In Chapter 1 we looked at the different food groups and nutrients that make up a healthy diet for a baby. The benefits of eating well include strong bones and teeth, plenty of energy for playing and learning, and a good immune system for fighting off infection. A nutritionally inadequate diet in the early years can have long-term irreversible effects on health, including brain development and heart health.

66 *My wife and I were fitness instructors so we are a bit aware of which foods to give Nancy for different nutrients. Fruit and veg are important, but people forget that other foods have vitamins too, like meat and eggs. Another thing we think about is fibre, to keep her regular. Fruit and vegetables are important but also foods like lentils.* 99
Rab, dad to Nancy, 21 months

> TIP If your baby is six months old and doesn't eat much because she can't feed herself, give her a little helping hand by spoon-feeding her too. By offering some mashed meals along with foods for self-feeding, she can learn about self-feeding while still getting the nutrients she needs.

Meeting a baby's nutritional requirements while trying to include her in family meals needs a little thought, since a healthy balanced diet for a baby is not the same as a good diet for an adult. For example, babies need to be given full-fat dairy products, while adults should go for the reduced-fat versions, as these are better for them. Another difference is that, while adults need to eat plenty of high-fibre foods, including wholegrain breakfast cereals, wholemeal bread and brown rice and pasta, babies don't.

How sharing meals works in practice

You may be thinking that it's all beginning to sound a little bit too complicated. But it isn't really that difficult, and the benefits are worth it. It just means sitting down to eat together whenever possible, and sometimes making a few adaptations to your baby's meal.

For example, if you are eating bran flakes, perhaps give your baby Weetabix instead. Your baby will still benefit from sitting with you so that you can eat together. Maybe you could both have some banana with your cereal then it doesn't seem so different. Wholemeal bread is still a good idea for both of you, as a baby who gets used to white bread might not switch to wholemeal very easily. When you have rice or pasta, perhaps you can vary between wholegrain and white varieties.

From the age of about two years, a child's diet can gradually be adapted, so that by the time children reach their fifth birthday they are eating the kind of foods that would be considered healthy for an adult. Part two contains lots more practical suggestions for you to try according to your baby's age.

How do you make sure your baby gets the nutrients she needs without 'making' her eat her meals?

Although you should never try to get a baby to eat when she doesn't want to, if she doesn't seem to be having much, it's worth looking at whether there's a reason for this and whether there's anything you can do. For example, if your baby never seems to eat breakfast, perhaps it is because she's just had a big milk feed. Most babies really enjoy a breastfeed or a bottle of milk when they wake up, so if breakfast comes soon after this, they may be too full to eat it. If breakfast is served an hour later, your baby may well enjoy it more.

Similarly, in the evening, a baby may be feeling too tired to eat if a meal is offered late. Having too much milk or juice during the day can also affect a baby's appetite for lunch and dinner, so can snacks just before a meal.

Sometimes small adjustments to your baby's routine can encourage better eating without the need for games or tricks.

4. Experimenting

Allow your baby to feed herself or handle food as soon as she shows any interest. The greater variety your baby has in her diet and the more often you try a food, the more chance there is that she'll eat it. By offering a wide variety of foods it can help avoid fussy eating later on. This doesn't mean your baby needs different types of exotic fruit or expensive ingredients from health food shops. You just need to offer all the different foods that you and your family eat, provided they're suitable for your baby's age, of course. This way your baby will get the opportunity to try a range of tastes and textures.

Some babies are more adventurous about trying new foods right from the beginning. Researchers say that a 'shared environment' is very important while babies are trying different foods. This basically means that children who see different foods around and have the chance to eat them more tend to like them more. For fruit and vegetables this is obviously a good thing, but for some other foods it's not!

Other research has found that the types of food that young children like to eat depends on 'modelling' and 'flavour conditioning'. In simple terms, this means babies and toddlers are more likely to eat something if they see someone else eating it and if they are given it lots of times so they can keep trying it.

> TIP Think twice about playing games – a few different studies have now shown that coaxing children to eat often results in them eating less rather than more.

If you eat together, your baby will have more opportunities to experiment with food. You can simply give your baby some of the same food you're having. This is easier than steaming four sticks of carrot or a spoonful of cabbage just for her. And if she sees you eating something, then this will encourage her to try it too.

It's good to allow a baby to taste lots of different foods, but it's also important to let her spit out food if she doesn't want it. This will give her the confidence to try a variety of foods in the early days. Later on, when your baby is eating well and able to understand more, you can start to talk about spitting and table manners. That's a parenting challenge for another day.

> 66 We travel to Spain and Italy a lot and I wanted Charlotte to eat what we do and see meal times as family times. At Christmas she was six months old and we'd just started baby-led weaning. She sat and ate, or rather licked and tasted, the same food as us. She loved being part of the occasion. We've just come back from Spain and Charlotte ate the same tapas we did. I know she will be fine for food wherever we go. 99
> **Daniella, mum to Charlotte, 10 months**

5. Flexibility

Some mums see cooking special meals for their baby as part of being a good parent, but there's nothing wrong with giving your baby the odd jar or pouch of commercially prepared baby food. Feeding your baby shouldn't be terribly time consuming or stressful.

It's also important to be flexible when it comes to purées versus finger foods. You may find that purées are good for a month or two then self-feeding naturally takes over. Or different approaches might suit different meals. Perhaps your baby could join in Sunday lunch with the family by feeding herself pieces of potato, chicken, carrot, broccoli and so on, cut into suitable chunks. Then on Monday it might be better to spoon-feed her a baby meal for lunch when you're out shopping. Another day your baby could be spoon-fed some parts of a meal but eat other bits with her hands. For example, you could give her shepherd's pie with a spoon, but she could have some broccoli spears to tackle herself. Or you could feed her chicken casserole, then let her have pear quarters for pudding. This involves some planning so that you make sure your baby has opportunities every day to feed herself and explore food, while still having some meals spoon-fed by you. Some days it may not be practical and that's absolutely fine. Just work out what is feasible for you.

> 66 *Ethan has enjoyed eating ever since he started. We mixed BLW with spoon-feeding and purées, which is something the BLW literature warned against, but it didn't seem to cause any confusion or problems. It often wasn't practical for Ethan to spend an hour feeding himself – for example in the mornings before I dropped him at the child minder – and he would always have something to feed and amuse himself with at the same time.* 99
> **Rebecca, mum to Ethan, 2 years**

The foods your baby wants to eat and the way she wants to get them in her mouth, either being spoon-fed or feeding herself, will change over time. As babies become more skilled, they will often demand more independence. If your baby decides that she wants to feed herself from now on, then try not to fight it. See it as a developmental milestone, rather than a problem. Often, very independent babies still prefer to be spoon-fed when they're very hungry or too tired to be chasing food around. You might find that spoon-feeding is easier in certain situations too, for example on a long drive or if you're eating at a friend's house.

Sometimes it will work well for you to eat the same food as your baby, but sometimes it won't. Even if it's not possible for evening meals, try to avoid getting into the habit of thinking in terms of 'baby food' and 'adult food' and always feeding your baby at a different time to yourself. If you think flexibly, you'll find there are often situations when you can eat together – lunchtimes and weekends are usually easier.

How to do it

If you choose to take a balanced approach to weaning, think about your baby as an individual when you are trying to decide the best time to start. Remember the official advice for the UK is to begin at around six months and the European advice is at four to six months. All the official guidelines state that babies should be considered on a case-by-case basis, so provided your baby is over four months old, the decision is up to you. You can look out for signs of readiness (see p8) and your health visitor should be able to help you decide.

How exactly you start is also up to you. Some people think it's important for a baby's first experience of food to be with pieces they can hold themselves rather than purées. If you want to start this way, that's great; but many parents don't feel comfortable doing this when their baby has only ever had milk before. They would rather start with a smooth purée and take things more gradually, which is absolutely understandable. There's no real evidence that one way is better than the other, so try either one – or, better still, try both and see how it goes.

> TIP As weaning progresses, you can introduce more variety in terms of flavours and textures, and this can be done as quickly or as slowly as you and your baby are comfortable with.

There is more about what to introduce, and when, and exactly how to go about things in Part two. There you'll see the different stages of weaning and get all the practical advice you'll need as your baby progresses.

Parents' top tips for a balanced approach

- If you get your baby used to a mixture of BLW and purées, you can feed her proper dinner at home but she can have a sandwich when you're out – much easier than trying to heat up casserole.
- Having a dog to help clear up the mess on the floor helps!
- Buy some flax meal (ground flax seeds). If you roll a banana in it, then it's not too slippery and your baby can hold it more easily. It's also good for mixing with foods such as porridge, and it gives a hearty nutty flavour.
- If you do BLW and a bit of spoon-feeding, you can give a bigger range of food – things like hot oat cereal, custard and rice pudding.
- Babies always think you're eating something better than they've got, so put some of their food onto your own plate to encourage them to eat it.
- Have a banana in a 'Break glass in case of emergency' box. They're just brilliant.

5

Buying the best food for your baby

Throughout the weaning process, and beyond, you'll have lots of decisions to make about the best foods to buy. This can be something of a minefield.

Consumers spend an average of just five seconds reading each food label in the supermarket, and parents of young children probably spend even less time than this. When time is limited, even nutritionists find it difficult to go through the small print on food labels and work out which are the healthiest products. The information in this chapter is intended to make choosing food as easy as possible.

Bought baby food

When you look down the baby aisle in your local supermarket you might be surprised at how much it can cost to feed a very small person. Baby food manufacturers would have us believe babies can only eat foods marketed specifically at them, but this isn't the case. In fact, many foods sold for babies contain exactly the same ingredients as those aimed at adults. Some products, such as organic fruit purées, can offer reasonably good value for money, but for others such as baby pasta, you're just paying more for a smaller bag.

The content of foods sold for babies and children under three is tightly regulated. There are strict rules about what manufacturers can put in, so the salt and sugar content of 'meals' is limited. (Incidentally, the same rules don't apply to 'snacks'.) Food additives, such as artificial colours and sweeteners, are not allowed in meals, and the level of pesticide residues must be virtually zero. This doesn't mean feeding your baby solely on jars is a good idea, but if you give the odd jar there's certainly nothing to feel guilty about. There are advantages and disadvantages to giving a baby commercially prepared meals.

Advantages

- You know your baby is getting a meal designed to meet her nutritional needs, whereas if the family is eating something like ready-made lasagne, your baby will get too much salt.
- They're convenient when you're out and about, as they don't have to be kept refrigerated, and, as long as your baby doesn't mind, they can be eaten cold instead of being reheated.
- When you're busy, they're a good stand-by.
- Some are very tasty and might be as good as home cooking.

TIP Jars, pots and pouches of fruit purée taste like they're homemade, contain nothing but fruit and can save you time, but not necessarily money.

Disadvantages

- They are more expensive than home cooking.
- Most are very sweet – even if spinach or broccoli is the first food mentioned on the label, the small print may reveal that something sweet (like apple) makes up 75% of the contents, compared with less than 10% broccoli. This may appeal to babies' natural preference for sweet flavours, but it doesn't encourage them to accept a range of flavours.
- They always taste the same, whereas homemade shepherd's pie or spaghetti is never exactly the same as last time.
- Food in jars is cooked at a very high temperature to give it a long shelf life, but this caramelises the sugars in foods such as carrots and gives them an unnatural flavour compared with home cooking.

- They don't get your baby used to eating family food, which is an important part of the weaning process.
- It can be difficult to move babies from stage 1 meals to stage 2, whereas if you're puréeing food yourself you can make the transition to lumpier food more gradually by just puréeing the food slightly less.

> 66 I gave the girls jars and homemade food, puréed in a blender: things like squashes, sweet potatoes, parsnips, broccoli and carrot. They preferred jars, but even with the jars, they could be quite choosey. They might like something one day and go off it big time after that. 99
> **Adam, dad to Tallulah, 4 years and Daisy, 2 years**

Do they encourage an early start?

You might notice that some jars are labelled as being suitable for babies from four months old, which seems surprising when the government says that weaning should start at around six months. The reason for this is that baby food is labelled in accordance with a European Union Directive. The European Union is planning to review the labelling guidelines, but it's unclear when this will happen. Baby food manufacturers are probably in no hurry to re-label and lose sales.

Breakfast cereal

If you're buying a breakfast cereal for a baby who is under six months old, then it's best to choose one that is especially made for this age group. That way you can make sure it is gluten-free. From six months, your baby can also have Weetabix or Ready Brek or a similar own-brand cereal. These breakfasts are much lower in salt and sugar than other cereals such as corn flakes or Shreddies. They also tend to be reasonably priced.

> TIP Choose a breakfast cereal with added vitamins and iron. It's an easy way to boost your baby's intake of these essential nutrients. Most own-brand cereals are almost identical to the branded ones, and they're fortified just like the branded ones. However, the cheapest 'basics' ranges sometimes aren't.

Avoid breakfast cereals that are chocolate-flavoured, frosted with a sugar coating or have added honey or syrup. They contain much more sugar than your baby needs and can encourage a sweet tooth. High-fibre breakfast cereals, such as bran flakes or All-Bran, aren't suitable for babies or toddlers either. Not only do they contain fibre, which will fill a baby up and reduce mineral absorption, they also tend to have quite a lot of salt added to make them more palatable.

When it comes to breakfast cereals, it may surprise you to hear that organic varieties aren't necessarily better for babies. This is because foods that have nutrients like iron and vitamins added can't be classified as 'organic'. So if you do choose organic Weetabix-type cereals instead of normal varieties, they will not be fortified, and so your baby will be missing out on a good source of nutrients.

Remember that regular porridge oats and muesli are not fortified either, so if you're concerned about your baby getting enough iron, then giving her these every day probably isn't a good idea. However, they're fine occasionally or if your baby eats plenty of other iron-rich foods.

Bread

It's good to get babies used to wholemeal bread right from the start because it tastes quite different to white bread. Once a baby or toddler gets used to white, it can be hard to get her to change, and that is a shame since wholemeal is much healthier.

Bread can make a significant contribution to a baby's salt intake. One slice typically contains about 0.5g of salt, which is half the maximum amount a baby should have on any single day. Check the label on the bread you usually buy, and, when you go shopping, compare it with other breads. You'll find there is quite a bit of variation in the salt content, even among loaves that look pretty similar. Some breads contain about half as much salt as others, but because they aren't labelled 'low salt' or 'reduced salt', you can only tell by looking at the small print nutrition information. The same is true for pitta bread and chapatti.

> TIP Check out supermarket own-brand bread. You might expect better-known brands to be healthier, but cheap loaves often contain less salt. Take a look at the label.

Yogurt

There is an enormous range of yogurt and fromage frais for babies and children. These have a healthy image as they are made from milk and fruit, which are healthy foods for growing children. However, you need to be careful about which ones you choose, as some contain quite a bit of added sugar, which babies don't need.

It is very easy to make your own fruit yogurt by mixing natural yogurt with fruit purée. Then you know your baby is getting just these two ingredients, rather than 10 to 20 ingredients, including flavourings and colourings.

If you want to use little pots for convenience, then there are a few points to bear in mind. First, there is no benefit in buying 'baby' yogurt or fromage frais rather than regular versions, provided you buy those that are made with full-fat milk. They are smaller, which may be handy, but the ingredients don't offer any other advantages. Some have added vitamin D, but the government recommends that all under-fives have drops containing vitamin D anyway so it's not so important.

> TIP Don't buy a particular yogurt or fromage frais just because it 'contains calcium for strong bones'. All milk products contain calcium, which helps build strong teeth and bones, even if they don't make this claim on the packaging.

When you're trying to choose the best one for your baby, have a look at the list of ingredients and go for one where fruit appears before sugar or concentrated fruit juice (which is another form of sugar). Ingredients are listed in order of quantity, so if fruit comes before sugar, you know the yogurt is getting more of its flavour from the fruit than from the sugar.

Snack foods

Babies and toddlers need snacks because they have small stomachs, so they can't eat enough at one meal to see them through to the next. Although most need snacks twice a day, they certainly don't need treats twice a day.

Foods such as rusks and biscuits shouldn't be given every day as they encourage little ones to develop a sweet tooth. Traditional rusks are high in sugar. Even reduced-sugar varieties are sometimes 20% sugar, which is more than a jam doughnut.

The market in baby snacks has grown enormously in recent years, with many snacks boasting that they're completely natural and healthy. But even the manufacturers say, albeit in very small print or on their websites, that most of these snack foods aren't for everyday consumption. It doesn't make much, if any, difference whether they are sweetened with grape juice or normal white sugar. The grape juice concentrate added to cereal bars and biscuits is refined. This is done to remove the grape flavour and odour but it also removes the beneficial nutrients, basically leaving sugar.

> TIP Think of crisps and other snack foods as occasional treats, not everyday snacks. Even low-salt 'baby-friendly' ones. If you're buying a treat, then choosing one low in salt and additives is better than choosing a regular adult version.

Giving a baby commercially prepared snack foods is never good if it's a regular occurrence. It makes eating packaged food seem the norm. Even low-salt savoury snacks still taste artificial. The strong flavour in these kinds of products can make foods in their natural unprocessed state seem bland. If your baby gets used to having these products regularly, she will almost inevitably move on to snacks such as regular crisps and chocolate-covered biscuits.

For snacks between meals, it is best to give foods such as a banana or some plain rice cakes or breadsticks. That said, the occasional sweet biscuit or piece of cake is absolutely fine. In Part two, there are plenty of ideas for healthy snacks that are appropriate for your child's age and stage of development.

Rice cakes

When your baby is just starting to hold food and feed herself, you might find baby-sized rice cakes are a good idea. Once she gets more skilled, though, there's no reason you can't buy large rice cakes and break bits off.

> TIP Save money by buying regular rice cakes instead of baby ones – but make sure you buy the plain ones without any added salt. A normal 130g pack costs about a pound, which is the same price as a 50g pack of baby rice cakes.

Several companies now produce flavoured rice cakes, but most babies are happy with plain ones, and it seems pointless introducing them to something artificially flavoured. The flavourings may come from natural sources, but these natural flavourings have been highly concentrated and artificially added to the rice cake. There's nothing fundamentally wrong with them, but if you want to give your baby something fruit-flavoured, why not give her some fruit?

Pasta

When you're buying dry pasta to cook for your baby, you may be tempted by the bags of special 'baby-friendly' pasta. If you look on the list of ingredients, however, you might be surprised to find they contain exactly the same ingredients as regular pasta. The only significant difference is that they cost about twice the price.

True, they generally come in smaller pieces, and in shapes such as mini-shells or stars. However, in some cases you'll be disappointed to find that the pretty shapes can't be distinguished once the pasta is cooked. Also, if you're going to mush or chop up a meal anyway, the end result is going to be the same.

Fish

Fish is full of nutrients, including protein, iron and vitamin B12. White fish, such as haddock and cod, is a good source of iodine and selenium. Oily fish, like salmon and sardines, supplies vitamin D and beneficial omega 3 fatty acids (see p18). When you're buying fish, fresh or frozen varieties are a great option, but if you don't feel confident cooking it, or just for convenience and variety, tinned fish is good too.

> TIP Tinned tuna is just about the easiest fish for babies to start with. You can add it to a tomato-based pasta sauce or mix it with mashed potato or rice and vegetables.

When you're buying tuna, have a quick look on the label to check the salt content. If you choose tuna canned in oil or brine, you'll find these contain similar amounts, about 0.3g in quarter of a can (1g salt per 100g tuna). This is because tuna canned in oil also tends to have salt added to it. Tuna canned in water has slightly less, 0.25g per quarter can. Babies can have up to 1g of salt a day, and while tuna canned in water has slightly less salt than tuna canned in oil or brine, it's not going to make much of a difference. With other fish there can be a greater variation in salt content.

Tinned sardines and mackerel are oily fish. They're very easy to use mashed with other foods such as rice or potato, or as a dip or spread (see p153). Again, it's really worth looking at the label for the salt content as there is a great deal of variation – not just depending on what liquid it's canned in, but also between different brands. Sardines canned in spring water contain about 0.2% salt (0.2g salt per 100g drained sardines); those in brine contain a similar amount (0.3%); but those canned in oil or tomato sauce contain anywhere between 0.9% and 1.7%, depending on the brand. So either choose those tinned in spring water, or look at the nutrient information of the tin to select the lowest salt option.

It's best to avoid buying smoked fish for your baby if you can buy fresh, frozen or canned fish instead. This is because it contains much more salt. Smoked salmon is typically 3% to 4% salt, so a small 25g portion contains the maximum amount of salt your baby should be getting from all her food in a day. Kippers and smoked mackerel contain around 3% salt, smoked trout about 2%, and smoked haddock around 1%. If you think that a normal grilled or baked piece of salmon or mackerel contains less than a tenth of this amount, it makes sense to get these instead.

Top 10 healthy convenience foods

1. Bananas
2. Weetabix (or similar own-brand products)
3. Mini boxes of raisins
4. Ready Brek (or similar own-brand products)
5. Rice cakes (no salt)
6. Fruit pots
7. Breadsticks
8. Tinned fish
9. Cream cheese
10. Houmous

Organic food

If you usually eat organic food yourself, you've probably already decided it is the best thing for your baby. If you like the idea of organic, but find it too expensive, you may be debating whether it's worth the extra expense.

Organic food is an issue that seems to divide opinion, with the media talking up both sides of the argument. One day it seems organic food is healthier or tastier or generally better than other food. Then a new study is quoted saying organic food isn't as nutritious as regular food. And then there are those who claim that there's no difference at all. So before you start paying extra for organic food, it's worth looking at how it really differs from other food.

Organic food is produced to standards that are designed to be more 'natural'. This has benefits in terms of the environment and animal welfare, but some experts question whether the end product, the food, is really that different. Organic farmers are not permitted to use certain pesticides, so organic food contains fewer and lower levels of pesticide residues. It is not completely pesticide-free, as some pesticides are allowed, and it can pick up contamination from the general environment. But it does have far less. And since nobody wants their baby eating food covered in chemicals, surely organic food is best for weaning?

In fact, the Food Standards Agency says the level of pesticide residue in all foods (so that's normal food too) is monitored to ensure it stays below safe limits. So no food, whether organic or conventionally grown, should be contaminated with pesticides that can damage health. Furthermore, the level of pesticide residue permitted in baby food is even lower than for other foods – effectively zero. Having said that, the Soil Association says the safety limits are set for adults rather than children, and although pesticides are tested individually for safety, no one really knows the possible side effects of exposing babies to a cocktail of different chemical residues.

> 66 *I buy organic food for us adults when I can, but for making Archie's meals, I've always made sure everything is organic. It's better for him if he doesn't have pesticides, and it's better for the environment – it's a lifestyle choice. I've found it easiest to do the food shopping for him, then make big batches of food to put in the freezer for him – maybe a fish meal, a meat one and a veggie one.* 99
> **Charlotte, mum to Archie, 11 months**

Is it more nutritious?

Some parents choose organic food for their baby because they believe it is more nutritious. Although several studies have found organic produce to contain higher levels of certain nutrients, others have found no difference. In 2009, a committee reviewed all the studies published in the past 50 years, looking at the nutritional differences between organic food and other food.[2] They concluded that there were no significant differences between the amount of vitamins and minerals in organically produced foods and in those produced conventionally. The authors also looked at studies investigating whether people who ate organic food were healthier, and found no evidence of any health benefits. Sounds simple – but remember that so far only limited research has been carried out in this area.

But while it's debatable whether organic food is nutritionally better, it does differ from conventionally farmed food in certain other ways. It is not allowed to contain genetically modified (GM) ingredients. Animals reared for organic meat are not only treated better, but they don't have antibiotics routinely added to their feed, or receive hormones to make them grow faster. Also, the use of additives in processed organic foods is restricted. This means artificial colourings and flavourings are not added to organic food. However, it also means organic breakfast cereals cannot have iron or vitamins added, which most conventional cereals do, so they provide lower levels of these (see p88).

> **❝** *I made puréed fruit and vegetables for both boys when they were weaning, but I didn't usually buy organic ingredients. Organic food is so expensive and I know it's no better nutritionally. When I bought jars, I tended to buy organic ones though – there wasn't much difference in price and they often had nicer recipes.* **❞**
> **Caroline, mum to Luke, 4 years and Hugh, 3 years**

So, the evidence of any benefit in eating organic isn't clear-cut, despite what organic food manufacturers may have you believe. Some scientists argue that buying organic food is more of a lifestyle choice rather than an informed decision based on proven health benefits. The bottom line is that there may be benefits, but we just do not know at the moment. If you can afford to buy organic food, then you may decide it is worth it. If you can't, then it is certainly not something worth worrying about. It is far more important to ensure your child eats a nutritionally balanced diet that includes all the recommended foods, as the health benefits of this are well established.

Pick and mix

If you decide to buy some organic and some normal foods, then it's sensible to go organic for those foods that are more likely to have high levels of pesticide or herbicide residues: for example, apples, grapes and tomatoes. Residues are generally reduced when foods are processed, such as when they are canned or ground. This means there is less reason to choose organic when you're buying foods such as tinned tomatoes, pasta, apple juice and biscuits. Cooking also reduces the level of pesticide residues, so it may not be worth paying extra for organic potatoes and onions, or other foods that are going to be cooked. It is more likely to make a difference if you are buying fruit or salad ingredients that are going to be eaten raw.

> ### Warning – organic doesn't mean healthy!
> Just because a food is organic, it doesn't mean it is good for your baby. So try not to be fooled by pictures of blue skies and golden wheat swaying in the wind. Organic sugar is still bad for a baby's teeth, and organic sausages are just as likely to contain too much salt and saturated fat as other sausages.

Seasonal eating

When you buy seasonal food, it is usually fresher and cheaper. This is because it has not been transported as far, or stored for as long, as other food. Most foods are now available throughout the year, but this involves crops being 'forced', which uses more chemicals to get them to grow or ripen when they wouldn't naturally.

> TIP Buy fruit and vegetables that are in season. They've been harvested at their peak and have the most flavour and nutrients. This means they're tastier and healthier. It's also better for the environment.

Another advantage of eating foods that are in season is that it can help the whole family have a more varied diet, rather than getting stuck in a food rut. It is very easy to give babies and young children the same food all the time, because you know they will eat it. But it is good to try new things too. You never know if they will like beetroot, cauliflower or rhubarb if you don't try them. Going to a market together and coming home with something that looks a bit different is a good way of encouraging your baby to be an adventurous eater.

What's in season when?

Season	Vegetables	Fruit	Other foods
Spring	New potatoes, asparagus, broccoli, cauliflowers, spinach and kale	Rhubarb	Lamb and pollack
Summer	Tomatoes, aubergine, broad beans, peas, courgettes and beetroot	Redcurrants, raspberries, strawberries and other soft fruit	Beef, coley and salmon
Autumn	Sweetcorn, leeks, pumpkins and squashes	Apples and pears	Cod and mackerel
Winter	Brussels sprouts, carrots, parsnips and swedes	Apples, dates and clementines	Herring and mackerel

Part two
The stages of weaning

In Part two we go through the different stages of weaning. Starting with stage 1, when your baby will have her first taste of solids, and ending with 'toddlers and beyond', when she'll be eating pretty much the same things as you.

Each chapter for each stage of your baby's weaning includes:

- what you can expect from your baby
- what you should be feeding her and how
- sample feeding plans
- recipes
- practical tips.

6

Stage 1:
four to six months

Your baby's first taste of solids may be carefully planned, or it might just happen before you have had time to think about it. Some babies start when they grab someone else's food or are given something to chew on by an older brother and sister. You may be happy to start by just giving your baby a taste of whatever it is you're eating, and that's fine.

If you prefer to plan things, this chapter includes step-by-step guidelines to help you through the first meals. You will probably have decided by now that your baby is ready for solids, but if you're at all unsure, then take another look at p8.

You may also have chosen which method of weaning you'd like to try first: the baby-led weaning (BLW) way with whole pieces of food, or giving your baby some purées, at least to begin with.

> TIP If you like the idea of starting with finger foods but you're at all worried, then begin with purées. Eating should be a positive experience, and if you're stressed it won't be. You can give finger foods in a few days' or weeks' time, once you've seen how your baby is coping and you're feeling more confident.

Don't forget that babies are all individuals, so do try to keep an open mind and see what works best for you and your baby. It would be simpler for us all if there were one correct weaning method guaranteed to work for every baby, but that isn't the case. If things don't go as you'd expected, try to stay positive and remember that most problems are only temporary and babies soon move on.

> **❝** *I started weaning my first son at three months and the second at four months. Then it was five months for Eleanor and six for the younger two. I don't think age made any difference to how things went. With Agnes it was really easy and I thought 'I've cracked this whole thing', but Martha was more difficult than any of the others. I felt the least in control with her and it was really frustrating trying to get her to eat.* **❞**
> **Kathryn, mum to Daniel, 22 years, Francis, 9 years, Eleanor, 7 years, Agnes, 4 years and Martha, 2 years**

In this chapter, we're going to start by looking at how to give your baby her first meal and when to introduce new foods. This advice applies to all babies – both breastfed and bottle-fed, and whether you favour purées or BLW. Next there are guidelines for mums who are concerned about how to manage breastfeeds around weaning. As we go through the stages of weaning, you'll see when bottles should be dropped as solids increase, but breastfeeding mums sometimes find this more complicated. Then we'll go through exactly how to prepare purées and finger foods, and how to give them to your baby.

If you're going to start with finger foods, you might want to skip the purées section for now. You can always come back to it if you decide to offer purées as well. The finger foods section is relevant to *everyone*, because, however you start the weaning process, it's a good idea to give your baby some opportunities to eat finger foods as well.

The first meal

When you and your baby are ready to start weaning, choose a time when you are both feeling relaxed and happy. A quiet afternoon is the ideal time.

It's up to you whether you want to start with some purée or a piece of food. Either way, make sure your baby isn't too tired or hungry to begin with. Some parents see their baby's first mouthful of solids as an exciting milestone, while others face it with fear, worrying how their baby will react. If this is the case, your baby is likely to pick up on your feelings, so try to be as calm as possible, and enjoy it!

On day one, the first thing to do is get the food ready (we'll talk about which are the best foods to begin with on p107). Then give your baby her usual milk feed, either a breastfeed or a bottle. When she's had about half of what she'd normally take, you can try offering the solids you've prepared. This way, hopefully, she'll still want to eat but won't be quite so hungry. If you find that she gets distressed when you stop the milk feed, then forget the idea for now and let her have as much milk as she wants. You can try again when she's finished or a bit later on. Some babies take to solids very quickly, but others take a while to get used to having anything other than milk.

> TIP Make sure your baby is sitting up straight, either in a highchair or on your lap. That way she'll be less likely to choke, and will be better able to explore the food and feel in control.

66 *I started weaning Aislinn when she was six months old, following the advice I'd been given. But Aidan still wasn't sleeping through at five months, so I started giving him some cereal, thinking it might fill him up a bit and help him last through the night. He seemed ready and took it easily, and although it didn't help his sleeping, I knew it wasn't doing him any harm.* 99
Trina, mum to Aislinn, 3 years and Aidan, 15 months

> ## What if they don't want to eat?
>
> Please don't panic if your baby is not interested in food just yet. Remember all babies are different, and perhaps your baby isn't ready, even though you are. Go back to p8 to see the signs your baby may give you to show you she's ready.
>
> If you're convinced she's ready, or she's reached six months, try a different time of day, or a different food. It may be that she wasn't in the mood, or she was tired.
>
> If you're starting when your baby is four months old, consider waiting a few weeks, or a month, and trying again.
>
> Whatever you do, don't get disheartened, and take it at your baby's pace.

Introducing new foods

In the first days or weeks of weaning, it is better if you don't give lots of new foods all at once. Then if your baby has any kind of reaction, it's easier to identify the cause. It is particularly important to go slowly if your baby is nearer four months than six months old when you begin.

Once your baby reaches six months, there's no need to be quite so cautious, and you can use your common sense. There is no need at this stage to introduce one vegetable at a time and leave days before giving the next new one.

If you have allergies in your family, then you will need to be particularly careful about introducing higher-risk foods, such as nuts and eggs. There is more about this in Chapter 11 on allergies (see p198), but if you're at all worried talk to your GP or health visitor. The theory that babies will avoid foods that they are allergic to is completely unfounded. It probably happens sometimes, and when it does it sticks in people's minds, but it is certainly not something to rely on.

TIP If you're concerned about offering any particular new foods, then do it in the afternoon rather than in the evening, especially if you have a family history of allergies. This way it is easier to see how your baby reacts and to get medical help or advice if you need it.

Try to introduce your baby to plenty of new foods and also swap around the foods you give her every day. If you freeze food this can be done fairly easily, and it's even better if she also gets to try the meals eaten by the rest of the family. Although it's good to introduce new foods one at a time, varying what you give your baby every day is beneficial right from the start.

A balanced diet for a four to six-month-old baby

In the next three chapters, looking at older babies, we'll be considering how to get a good balance of nutrients. At this stage, however, you don't need to worry too much about your baby's nutrient intake. You are simply getting her used to eating something other than milk and trying different flavours. So there is no need to plan how many portions of fruit and vegetables to offer each day, or how to make sure she gets enough protein or carbohydrate.

Throughout the weaning process, it's important to remember that the objective isn't just to supply nutrients – weaning is also about helping your baby develop a healthy attitude to food. And this is particularly true in these early days.

You may be wondering how big these meals should be, and the answer is that you should be guided by your baby's appetite. Most parents soon discover how much their baby is likely to eat at each meal. It's quite normal for babies to eat very little one day and much more the next, but you'll get a general idea. If you're starting with purées frozen in ice-cube trays, you might initially make a meal of just one cube of carrot and one of potato. If this is all eaten up, you'll know to prepare two cubes of each next time.

> ❝ I started weaning Isaac at 20 weeks and it's been going well. I've enjoyed making all the food for him fresh, and have found it very rewarding when he gobbles it all up. It takes him a while sometimes to get the hang of it, but when he does, his mouth opens wide for the spoon. I was confused and worried that I was starting weaning too early, but he eats it, so I guess that means he was ready for it. ❞
> **Sarah, mum to Isaac, 5½ months**

What to do if you're breastfeeding

If you're breastfeeding your baby at the moment, you may find it a bit more complicated to know when to cut down on feeds. With bottle-fed babies, it's relatively easy to follow a timetable, but with breastfed babies it's not so simple. The first thing to say is that you should carry on for as long as it suits you both. Sometimes mums worry about how to fit weaning, which they see as something that should be done in a more controlled way, around breastfeeding, which they might be doing as and when their baby wants it during the day and night

A five to six-month-old baby who hasn't started solids will typically be having about five breastfeeds a day: first thing, mid-morning, lunchtime, mid-afternoon and bedtime. Quite a few babies are still having an additional feed during the night and some are feeding on demand day and night.

> ❝ I feel totally confused about breastfeeding and weaning and when to drop feeds. I feed on demand, but I'm not sure if I should stop so that I don't overfeed her once I start weaning. I'm not sure about giving her water either as she won't take a bottle. I generally feel quite uncertain about what I'm doing and there seems to be so much conflicting information, even the health visitors at my clinic all give different advice. ❞
> **Lara, mum to Vanessa, 6 months**

To begin with, while your baby is getting used to having some food, it's best to carry on with your usual breastfeeds. If you follow the weaning advice and slowly start offering your baby more foods, you'll probably find she settles into a pattern with fewer breastfeeds. You may also find that from about six months she gets more interested in other things going on around her, which means she gets distracted more easily when she's breastfeeding.

> TIP Once your baby is having lunch every day, you can drop the lunchtime feed. Then as she eats more you can drop the mid-morning feed too. By the time she reaches six or seven months and is having three meals a day, then three good feeds each day should be enough.

Establishing a good routine of meals and feeds may take a few weeks, but if you find it doesn't happen naturally and you're feeding all day, then try to stretch the periods between feeds by going out or playing with your baby. Hopefully by doing this, her feeding pattern will start to look more like those in the sample meal plans (see p113). Babies who continue to have frequent breastfeeds each day, just like those who have too much formula, tend to eat less and may not get all the nutrients they need, particularly iron. Having said that, use your common sense and maternal instinct to decide what's best. For example, if your baby has a cold or if she just wants to feed and you think she's not well, then wait a few days before trying to make any changes to your feeding routine. If you're worried about your baby's iron levels, you could get a packet of baby porridge with added iron to put your mind at rest.

Continuing to breastfeed while you introduce solids can have great health benefits for your baby. For example, research shows that babies might have an increased chance of developing coeliac disease if they are not being breastfed when gluten is introduced to their diet. Breastfeeding while wearing may also protect against diabetes. So if you and your baby are happy to continue breastfeeding, that is wonderful.

Purées

If you're going to start weaning in the traditional way by spoon-feeding your baby, you can begin by offering her baby rice or puréed fruit or vegetables. Baby rice is popular because it has a very bland flavour and when it's mixed with your baby's usual milk, it doesn't taste very different.

Start by making it up to a very thin consistency and offering just a spoonful. Then you can offer more baby rice, with less milk added, so that it is slightly thicker, more like a runny yogurt.

> TIP If you make up baby rice with breast milk, you may find that, although you mix it to a reasonable consistency, when you leave it for a minute it turns into a thin liquid. This is because of the enzymes in your breast milk. You can't stop this happening, so just add more baby rice and mix it to a good consistency again.

Some babies start with foods, such as broccoli, that have a much stronger flavour, and they seem to get on fine. Some parents think it is best to get babies used to vegetables first, before they have any fruit, to prevent them developing a sweet tooth, but it's up to you.

If your baby is less than six months old, then you should do all this very gradually. If she's coped well with the first few fruits and vegetables, without any stomach upset, constipation or allergic reaction, then other foods can be introduced more quickly.

If you want to begin weaning with fruit or vegetables, below you'll find a list of the best first purées.

Good first purées

Carrot	Sweet potato
Apple	Broccoli
Butternut squash	Cauliflower
Parsnip	Avocado
Pear	Apricot

At first, it is good to make purées of single vegetables such as carrot or broccoli. Your baby then has the opportunity to taste the food on its own. Later, you can also mix these vegetables with other foods to make more interesting dishes. For example, if you cook a batch of carrot, your baby can have it on its own, mixed with baby rice or mixed with parsnip and swede.

Provided she's six months old, she could also have it with cheese and potato or with pasta. Remember: instead of cooking batches of food just for your baby, it is less hassle to just make extra when you're preparing the family meal so there is some leftover for the freezer.

> TIP If your baby is prone to constipation, pear may be the best food to start with – it is less likely than baby rice to cause a problem. There is more about constipation on p220.

How to offer purées

- Allow plenty of time, especially at first, so that your baby doesn't feel rushed and can enjoy the experience.
- Make the food slightly warm, not cold from the fridge but definitely not as hot as you might eat it yourself.
- Use a shallow spoon and make the food fairly runny – that way it'll be easier for her to get the food off the spoon.
- Show your baby the spoonful of food and wait for her to open her mouth. Then try putting the spoon to the inside of her bottom lip so that she can take the food.
- Let your baby take the food into her mouth herself, rather than you tipping the food off the spoon at the back of her mouth. By doing it herself, she'll be less likely to choke and better able to handle lumps.
- If the food comes out of her mouth, but she's happy, then just try to spoon it in again. This isn't a sign that she doesn't want it. It could just be that she hasn't yet learned how to push it to the back of her mouth to swallow.
- If she wants to touch the spoon or the dish with her hands then let her. Also, if she grabs the spoon then let her have it, just make sure you've got another one to use yourself. You could even dip her spoon in the food too.

You may find she gets frustrated between spoonfuls. This can be because she's used to her food, which up to this point has been milk, coming in a continuous stream. Try to resist the temptation to spoon the food in quickly. It is better for her to get used to eating more slowly.

If your baby doesn't seem to want the food, don't worry. At this stage, your baby is just getting used to the idea of having something to eat other than milk. It's important that she doesn't start to see meal times as upsetting.

> TIP Even if your baby seems keen to eat more than a couple of spoonfuls, it is wise to start with a small amount so that her digestive system can get used to it. After a few days, you can offer her more if she wants.

Basic vegetable or fruit purée

The method for making vegetable or fruit purée is basically the same whatever vegetable or fruit you choose. The two exceptions are pear, which goes too watery when cooked this way, and potato, which turns gluey. Separate methods for puréeing these are given below.

Take one of the following:

Carrots (peeled and diced)
Parsnip (peeled and diced)
Sweet potato (peeled and diced)
Broccoli (washed and chopped)
Apple (peeled, cored and chopped)
Cauliflower (washed and chopped)
Butternut squash (skin and seeds removed, then diced)
Plus 100ml water

Preparation time: 25 minutes
Pans: 1
Storage: Suitable for freezing; keeps in the fridge for up to 24 hours.
Servings: As a rough guide, a 500g bag of carrots, parsnips or sweet potatoes produces enough purée to fill about two ice-cube trays. The same goes for an average whole broccoli or a small cauliflower. To start with, your baby might eat just one or two cubes, so two ice-cube trays should hold enough for about 14 meals.

- Put the water in a pan and bring to the boil. Add the vegetable, put a lid on the pan and bring back to the boil. Simmer for about 10 minutes until soft, checking that the water doesn't boil away and adding a little more water if necessary.
- Purée with as much of the cooking water as necessary until smooth. If your baby is six months old, you shouldn't need to make purées completely smooth, as babies this age can often cope with lumpier food.

Tips

- Spoon the cooked purée into ice-cube trays straight away, as it will cool down quickly like this.
- When cool, put the tray into a freezer bag or cover it with cling film and put it in the freezer.
- Once it's frozen, you can pop the cubes of purée out and put them into a freezer bag, labelled with the date and contents.
- When you are giving the purée to your baby, you can add a little expressed milk or formula milk if you wish.

Potato purée

Potatoes (e.g. Maris Piper, King Edward or Desiree)
Water
Optional – milk (breast or formula)

Preparation time: 25 minutes
Pans: 1
Storage: Suitable for freezing; keeps in the fridge for up to 24 hours.

- Peel the potatoes and cut into chunks. Place them in a pan with just enough water to cover them.
- Put the lid on and bring to the boil, then turn down the heat and simmer for about 20 minutes or until tender. Drain the water but keep some in a jug.
- Mash the potato with a fork or a potato masher. If you have a mouli you could use this. Add as much of the cooking water as you need to make a smooth purée.

Tips

- Portion out the purée for freezing, as described above.

- Add your baby's usual milk to the purée if you wish. If your baby is over six months old you can use cows' milk.

Pear purée

Pears
Baby rice

Preparation time: 25 minutes
Pans: 1
Storage: Suitable for freezing; keeps in the fridge for up to 24 hours.

- Peel and core the pears and chop into chunks. Place in a pan, without water, over a low to medium heat.
- Once the pan gets hot, turn it down low and simmer until the fruit is soft. You'll find that quite a bit of liquid comes out of the pears.
- Purée with a blender until smooth and allow to cool slightly. Add baby rice, a little at a time, until the mixture is about the same consistency as yogurt.
- You can then portion out the purée for freezing, as described above.

Going bananas

Bananas are popular with most babies because of their natural sweetness. They are best mashed with a fork rather than puréed, otherwise they tend to go too slimy. Don't worry about making them completely smooth, as this can be a good way of introducing slightly lumpier food to your baby.

Mixed vegetable purées

Once your baby has had some single vegetables puréed, you can try some combinations such as:

- carrot and swede
- carrot, swede and parsnip
- carrot and cauliflower
- sweet potato and cauliflower
- carrot and potato

- broccoli and potato
- cauliflower, broccoli and potato
- pea and potato
- potato, broccoli and peas.

You can make these by mixing together the single vegetable purées you have already made. This is the best thing to do for purées that include potato. For those that just include vegetables such as carrot and swede, you can cook them together if you prefer.

Mixed fruit purées

Once your baby has tried some single fruit purées you could offer the following for a bit of variety:

- banana and pear
- apple and pear
- apple and mango
- banana and peach
- apple and melon.

TIP At first, apples are best cooked, but soft fruits like ripe pear, bananas and peaches can just be peeled and mashed with a fork.

Sample meal plans

You don't have to follow a meal plan, but some parents find them useful for giving them an idea about what to give their baby at different stages. Remember these are just examples – if you'd rather start with pear or a vegetable purée instead of baby rice, that is absolutely fine.

When you look through the sample plans, you'll see that if you start weaning at six months you don't need to take things as slowly as you would if you'd started earlier. You should introduce a variety of foods more quickly and increase the number of meals eaten each day more quickly too.

> ## Portion control
> Don't worry too much at this stage about how much your baby is eating. Babies may start by eating just a teaspoonful but increase to having a few tablespoonsful. Be guided by them.

Stage 1 meal plan: if you are starting to wean your baby at four months old

Week	Morning	Mid-morning	Lunch	Mid-afternoon	Evening
Week 1	Milk feed	Milk feed	Milk feed plus baby rice	Milk feed	Milk feed
Week 2	Milk feed	Milk feed	Baby rice and pear or carrot	Milk feed	Milk feed
Week 3	Milk feed	Milk feed	Baby rice and butternut squash, carrot or pear	Milk feed	Pear or apple Milk feed
Week 4	Milk feed	Milk feed	Baby rice and butternut squash, carrot or pear	Milk feed	Pear or carrot Milk feed
Week 5 (five months old)	Milk feed	Milk feed	Carrot and potato, or same as last week Apple or pear	Milk feed	Apple or pear and baby rice Milk feed

Week 6	Milk feed	Milk feed	Parsnip or swede and potato, or same as last week Apple, pear or banana	Milk feed	Vegetable with baby rice or potato Apple or pear Milk feed
Week 7	Milk feed	Milk feed	Vegetable with rice or potato Fruit as before	Milk feed	Vegetable with baby rice or potato Apple or pear Milk feed
Week 8	Milk feed Porridge	Milk feed	Parsnip or other vegetable with potato Mango or pear	Milk feed	Vegetable with baby rice Apple or banana Milk feed
Week 9 (at least six months old)	Milk feed Weetabix or porridge Fruit	Milk feed	As before with meat or fish Fruit	Milk feed Rice cake	Vegetable with potato Fruit Milk feed

Stage 1 meal plan: if you are starting to wean your baby at five months old

Week	Morning	Mid-morning	Lunch	Mid-afternoon	Evening
Week 1	Milk feed	Milk feed	Baby rice for three days Baby rice and pear for next four days Milk feed	Milk feed	Milk feed
Week 2	Milk feed	Milk feed	Carrot or broccoli with baby rice or potato Apple or pear	Milk feed	Apple or pear Milk feed

Continued over page

Continued from overleaf

Week	Morning	Mid-morning	Lunch	Mid-afternoon	Evening
Week 3	Milk feed	Milk feed	Broccoli, carrot or parsnip with potato or sweet potato Banana or other fruit	Milk feed	Vegetable with baby rice Fruit Milk feed
Week 4	Milk feed Porridge	Milk feed	Vegetable with baby rice or potato Banana or pear	Milk feed	Vegetable with baby rice or potato Apple or pear Milk feed
Week 5 (at least six months old)	Milk feed Weetabix or porridge Fruit	Milk feed	Vegetable with rice or potato plus meat or fish Fruit	Milk feed Rice cake	Vegetable with rice or potato Fruit Milk feed

Stage 1 meal plan: if you are starting to wean your baby at six months old

Day/week	Morning	Mid-morning	Lunch	Mid-afternoon	Evening
Day 1	Milk feed	Milk feed	Baby rice Milk feed	Milk feed	Milk feed
Day 2	Milk feed	Milk feed	Baby rice and apple Milk feed	Milk feed	Milk feed
Day 3	Milk feed	Milk feed	Baby rice and pear Milk feed	Milk feed	Baby rice Milk feed
Day 4	Milk feed	Milk feed	Baby rice and carrot Apple Milk feed	Milk feed	Baby rice and pear Milk feed

Day 5	Milk feed	Milk feed	Carrot and potato Apple Milk feed	Milk feed	Baby rice and pear Milk feed
Day 6	Milk feed	Milk feed	Carrot and potato Banana Milk feed	Milk feed	Carrot and baby rice Pear Milk feed
Day 7	Milk feed	Milk feed	Broccoli and potato Fruit Milk feed	Milk feed	Carrot and potato Fruit Milk feed
Week 2	Milk feed Porridge or Weetabix Fruit	Milk feed	Meat or fish with vegetable and baby rice or potato	Milk feed Rice cake	Vegetable with baby rice or potato Fruit Milk feed

Worried about gagging or choking?

Babies have a more sensitive gag reflex than adults and will start to gag before food reaches the back of their throats and the risk of choking becomes imminent. So try not to panic or look alarmed. Most babies will bring the food back to the front of their mouth and continue eating. Soon they'll learn to chew food more carefully. There's more information on what you can do to prevent this happening on p32.

Finger foods

You can start to give your baby finger foods right from day one of weaning if you want to. Alternatively, you can start with baby rice and puréed fruit or vegetables, and then give finger foods a try. Or you can use both at the same time.

If your baby is six months old, she is probably ready to have finger foods. At around this age, babies start learning to grasp objects in their fists and bring them to their mouths. You'll notice this with toys and other things, including your baby's hands. Your baby is likely to be teething too, even if you can't yet feel or see any teeth emerging. This can make babies want to bite on things even more, for relief. All of which makes six months of age a good time to start introducing your baby to foods for self-feeding. Giving her finger foods will encourage her to chew, whether or not she has any teeth yet. It will also help her start to learn about how different foods feel, and start her off on the journey to independent eating.

> 66 *Edith had purées and she's a good eater, but I didn't have time for cooking and puréeing with Beatrix so I tried BLW. She loved it and now Humphrey does too. He can't sit up on his own, but loves being propped up in a highchair at the table with sticks of food while the girls are eating. He's at the tasting, grimacing and spitting stage, though I think a few morsels of pear have actually been swallowed.* 99
> **Jules, mum to Edith, 5 years, Beatrix, 2 years and Humphrey, 6 months**

Just as vegetables and fruit are good to start with for purées, they are also the best first foods for self-feeding. You'll find lots of products in the shops that are labelled as ideal first finger foods, but products such as rusks and biscuits, whether they're flavoured with sugar, honey or grape juice, will encourage your baby to develop a sweet tooth. Likewise, giving your baby packets of savoury snacks will not help her develop a taste for naturally healthy foods (see p90).

> TIP Cook vegetables until they are soft enough for your baby to eat but not so soft that they break up when she holds them in her fist.

Sticks of vegetable are good to start with and can be steamed, boiled or roasted. As with purées, some parents prefer to get their baby used to eating vegetables before they introduce fruits, which obviously have a sweeter flavour. When you serve fruit like apples and pears, you can either offer them whole and let your baby have a go, or you can cut them up to make them more baby-friendly.

First finger foods

- Cooked broccoli and cauliflower florets
- Cooked green beans, mange tout or sugar snap peas
- Steamed or roasted vegetable sticks, e.g. carrot or parsnip
- Cooked baby sweetcorn
- Boiled or roast potatoes
- Pieces of banana
- Plain, salt-free rice cakes

Steamed or boiled vegetable sticks

Use any of the following:

Carrots (peeled)
Parsnips (peeled)
Sweet potato
Plus 100ml water

Preparation time: 20 minutes
Pans: 1
Storage: Suitable for freezing; keeps in the fridge for up to 24 hours.
Servings: A medium carrot or parsnip will make 6–8 sticks.

- Wash the vegetables and peel as necessary. Then cut them into what look like fat chip-shaped pieces.
- These can be steamed if you have a steamer, otherwise put 100ml of water in a pan.
- Bring the water to the boil, then add the vegetables and simmer with the lid on until soft.

Tips

- Parsnips can be a bit stringy down the centre so you might need to cut them in quarters and remove this section. Or you can see how your baby copes and if necessary remove the centre during the meal.
- It is best to use only a little water when cooking, as this will ensure the vegetables retain as many of their vitamins as possible. Vitamin C and folic acid are lost very easily from vegetables if they are boiled.

- Make sure your pan doesn't boil dry. If you are left with some water at the end, keep it to use for making purées or other dishes, such as soup or pasta sauce.

Roast vegetable sticks

Use any of the following:

Carrots (peeled)
Parsnips (peeled)
Courgettes
Sweet potato (peeled or just scrubbed)
Aubergine
Beetroot (peeled)
Red, yellow or orange peppers (deseeded)
Potato (peeled)
Plus olive oil

Preparation time: 45 minutes (including 30–40 minutes in the oven)
Pans: 1 baking or roasting tray
Storage: These are best eaten when freshly cooked, but can be kept in the fridge for 24 hours. They can be put in the freezer, but will go a bit floppy when they're defrosted.
Servings: A medium carrot, courgette, pepper or parsnip will make 6–8 sticks. Other larger vegetables will make more.

- Preheat the oven to 220°C/425°F/gas mark 7.
- Wash the vegetables and peel if necessary.
- Cut the vegetables into fat chip shapes (about 5cm long) or other manageable pieces. For example, small beetroots can be cut into quarters and peppers can be sliced into strips. Bear in mind that when they are roasted, the vegetables will shrink slightly, so keep things quite chunky.
- Pour one tablespoon of oil into a food bag, add the vegetables and shake around until they are all covered in oil. Put the vegetables onto the baking sheet, place in the oven and roast for 30–40 minutes, turning occasionally.
- When the vegetables are soft, put them on kitchen paper towels to cool and absorb excess oil.

Green beans and sugar snap peas

Use any of the following:

> Green beans (sometimes called fine beans or dwarf beans)
> Mange tout
> Sugar snap peas
> Plus 100ml water

Preparation time: 20 minutes
Pans: 1
Storage: Suitable for freezing; keeps in the fridge for up to 24 hours.
Servings: Babies can be given a couple to start with, but can eat more if they wish.

- These vegetables are often de-stringed already when you buy them. If not, top and tail them and pull away any stringy fibres that may run down the side.
- You can then steam them or boil them in a small amount of water until soft.

Baked toast fingers

> Wholemeal bread

Preparation time: 22 minutes (including 20 minutes in the oven)
Pans: 1 baking tray
Storage: Keep in an airtight container for up to 5 days.
Servings: One slice of bread will make about 4 fingers.

- Preheat the oven to 160°C/325°F/gas mark 3.
- Take a slice of bread and cut off the crust, then cut into soldiers about 2cm wide. Place the fingers on a baking tray and bake for 20 minutes.
- Remove from the oven and leave to cool.

Tips

- These are only suitable for babies who are six months old or more.
- Bread cooked this way doesn't get mushed as easily as plain bread or toast.
- They are great for babies who are teething.

Fruit for finger food

Soft fruits such as pear and banana are ideal at the start of weaning. Some parents find that with some fruit it's better to leave the skin on, then it isn't squeezed and broken so easily.

- **Pears** can be given whole, or you can take a bite out, to make it easier for your baby to get a grip and get started on it. You could also cut it into quarters and remove the core and, if you wish, the skin.
- **Bananas** can be cut in half and peeled completely, or you can cut down the peel so that it is covering half the piece of banana and providing a 'handle' for your baby. After a while, babies learn how hard they can grip a banana so that it doesn't turn to mush.
- **Avocados** are best washed and then offered with a bit of skin on. If you cut the avocado into quarters and remove the stone, your baby can hold a piece and eat the flesh from the skin.
- **Mangos** can be eaten in the same way as avocados.
- **Grapes** and **cherry tomatoes** should be cut in half to avoid choking.
- **Melon** can be offered with the skin, or you can use a crinkle cutter to make hand-sized pieces that aren't quite so slippery.
- **Peaches** should be cut into quarters and have the stone removed.

Moving on

Once your baby has got used to eating a few different vegetables and fruit, you can introduce more flavours and textures whenever she seems ready. Remember that if she hasn't yet reached six months, there are certain foods that should be avoided (see p23).

If she's coping well, you can gradually increase the amount of solids she has by giving her more at each meal and moving up to three meals a day. It's good to start slowly if your baby hasn't yet reached six months, but after that you can begin to take her appetite as a guide to how much to give her.

If you are mainly spoon-feeding and your baby seems to eat quite fast and want more food, then you could give her more finger foods. As babies naturally have a sweet tooth, some will happily continue eating fruit purée until you stop giving it to them. Finger foods, such as slices of pear, banana or other fruit, take longer to eat and require more effort. If she's actually had enough, her body will have time to register this when she's eating more slowly, but if she does want more, she can still have it.

Once your baby is six months old, you can try offering a wider range of foods, including protein and iron-rich foods such as chicken and fish. By the time most babies are seven months old, they should be having breakfast, lunch and an evening meal, as well as having three or four milk feeds. Some may also have one or two snacks each day.

The lists below show new foods you can start to introduce from six months, along with the vegetables and fruits that your baby may already be eating.

More foods to include in purées and mashed meals

- Meat, chicken and fish
- Rice, noodles and pasta
- Lentils and pulses
- Scrambled eggs
- Full-fat dairy foods, such as cheese and yogurt

You can start mixing these foods with potato or vegetable purées that you are already making, or look at Chapter 7 for more ideas.

More finger foods for babies who are at least six months old

- Cubes of hard cheese, e.g. cheddar
- Toast fingers
- Strips of pitta bread or chapatti
- Slices of peeled raw apple
- Chicken legs or strips of brown chicken meat (breast meat may be too dry)
- Lamb or pork, as chops or as thin strips of meat

Milk and other drinks

When your baby is starting to eat solids, it is very important to give her water too (see p21). Use a cup to offer her sips of water during the meal right from day one of weaning, if not before. She might not take it at first, but keep trying. It's good to offer water between meals as well, especially in hot weather.

Milk is still very important to babies when they start to take solids. At first, your baby is unlikely to be getting many calories or much in the way of nutrients from food, so she needs breast milk or formula as usual. Until she is 12 months old, she will require 500–600ml of milk per day. This should be breast milk or infant formula, since cows' milk is not a suitable drink for babies under 12 months of age, although using small amounts in cooking is fine from six months.

Follow-on milk

Infant formula labelled as 'follow-on' milk or 'good night' milk is not suitable for babies under six months. You can start using it after that if you want to but there is no need. According to the NHS, there are *no* proven health benefits.

Some sceptics believe these products were only invented by baby food companies to get around the rules banning TV advertising of infant formula for babies under six months old.

Babies who are exclusively breastfed and don't have any formula need between three and five feeds a day from the age of six months. Remember that more milk is not necessarily better once a baby reaches six months. This is true whether it's breast milk or formula, as babies need to start getting more of the nutrients that solids can provide.

What to expect in your baby's nappy

When you start to give your baby solids you'll notice that her poo gradually begins to change in colour, texture and smell. Some parents are quite shocked when they're changing their baby's nappy and find everything looks different, so it's good to know what to expect and what's normal!

An exclusively breastfed baby typically has yellow poo that is sweet-smelling and loose but textured. The poo of a formula-fed baby, by contrast, is usually pale yellow or yellowish-brown, smellier and formed (more like adult poo).

When your baby first has some food, things tend to come out much as they went in. So if you start with puréed carrot, later that day (or the next day) your baby's poo may look a bit orange. Likewise, after broccoli her poo may be greenish. This is completely normal and it just takes your baby's digestive system a bit of time to adjust to coping with solids, rather than just dealing with milk. If you are just giving your baby finger foods, then changes in her nappy will let you know that she really is managing to eat something.

As your baby eats more over the next few weeks, her poo will become more solid and, unfortunately, it will become smellier. The changes are most noticeable in breastfed babies because to start with their poo is so unlike adult poo. It's quite normal to see bits, such as raisins, beans, seeds or tomato skin, in a baby's nappy as these things are harder to digest. However, if foods such as beans are coming out as they went in it means your baby isn't getting the nutrients they contain, so next time you give your baby beans it might be a good idea to mush them a bit.

> TIP To avoid your baby becoming constipated when she starts solids, take things slowly and give her plenty of water to drink.

If your baby starts to become constipated, avoid baby rice and bananas for a little while and instead give her pears, prunes and other fruit and vegetables. If you are switching from breastfeeding to formula this can also result in constipation, so it's important to make the transition slowly, over at least two weeks. Also, don't do it at the same time as starting to wean: this could make constipation even more likely.

If your baby's poo has any blood or mucous in it, or if you're worried that her poo doesn't look normal, then you should see your doctor or health visitor.

Practical tips to make the first stage easier

- Give your baby a weaning spoon to chew on and play with for a few days before you start weaning so she can become familiar with it. Then, when you give her solids, she'll only have to deal with the new texture of the food, instead of both the food and the spoon being new.
- Most unprocessed foods that you eat, including fruit and vegetables, are suitable for your baby too, so you don't need to make her special meals.
- When you're cooking vegetables for yourself, don't add salt, then your baby can have some and you don't have to cook for her separately.
- If you're making jacket potatoes, put one in for your baby. You can just scoop out some of the middle and mash it for her. You can even put the rest in the freezer for another day.
- Keep something in the freezer that your baby can eat when you're in a hurry.
- You can make a batch of dishes just for your baby, but you can also freeze portions of leftover vegetables from family meals.
- Whenever you're cooking vegetables for the rest of the family, make extra so that you can put some away for your baby to eat another day. That way your baby will get used to the foods the rest of the family usually eats.
- If you have cooking water left after boiling vegetables, keep it in ice-cube trays to use for stock another day (it's full of vitamins).
- If you find some meals very messy, give them to your baby in the evening. Then she can go straight from her highchair to her bath.

7

Stage 2:
seven to nine months

Your baby should now have had a chance to try some different foods and will hopefully have got used to having solids as well as milk. Whether you started weaning at four, five or six months, your baby now needs to be having three meals a day. You should be giving her a wide range of foods, including starchy foods and protein-rich foods, as well as the vegetables and fruits she started with.

If you are only just starting to wean at this age, don't worry – take things slowly for a few days and see how your baby manages. You might be surprised how keen she is, even if you're feeling more cautious yourself. There is no need to offer smooth purées. You can go straight to providing the foods described here, which are appropriate for your baby's age and needs.

Between the age of seven and nine months, babies are growing and developing rapidly. Most babies this age can sit up without support, which makes meal times and eating a whole lot easier. They are also learning to manipulate objects in their hands more easily. Their pincer grip is developing and this enables them to pick up small objects between the thumb and forefinger.

> TIP Give your baby raisins, peas, grated apple or grated cheese so she can practise picking things up between her thumb and forefinger.

Getting hands-on

At this stage babies also start to pass objects between one hand and the other and are likely to have a few teeth coming through. All of these developmental changes mean babies can start to feed themselves more easily. You'll probably find that your baby's ability to feed herself will progress in fits and starts. You'll see her struggling one day, then suddenly notice she can do something new.

> 66 Will didn't want anything but baby rice until he was well into his seventh month, but now he enjoys all his food. My new breakthrough is a little blender with a plastic pot attached. Now he can have whatever I'm cooking, or leftovers, and I just add formula to make it runnier or baby rice to thicken it up a bit. It's saved money, and by trying lots of random foods, I hope it'll give him a wide palate of different subtle flavours. 99
> **Bee, mum to Eva, 9 years, Zola, 8 years, Elsa, 4 years and Will, 8 months**

At around seven to eight months, most babies really enjoy getting to grips with their food, so whether or not you offer many finger foods, your baby will probably start trying to handle what you give her, even purées. This is inevitably messy, but it shouldn't be discouraged. If you're wary about offering finger foods, then for starters you could try rice cakes. They don't turn to mush too quickly, as bread does, but they can be gummed or chewed quite easily. While younger babies need self-feeding foods to be bigger than their fists, at this age it is not always necessary. As your baby becomes better at manoeuvring foods in her hands, she'll be able to cope with pieces that vary in size and texture.

Later on, when your baby is getting more skilled and is enjoying feeding herself with her hands more, you can load her spoon with dishes such as fish pie, which are mushy, and she can start learning to spoon-feed herself. The more opportunities she has for practising, the faster she'll learn. However, for the time being, you may find it's better for you to continue doing the spoon-feeding when it comes to runnier foods, such as porridge or yogurt. Give your baby a spoon to have a go too, and when she's ready to do it alone she'll let you know.

> 66 *My first two daughters had purées, and I started weaning Molly in the same way, but after a few days she only wanted to eat what I was eating. By chance, I found a leaflet about baby-led weaning (BLW) and it made sense to me, so I tried it. It worked really well for her and I'm planning to do the same with Alice. I'm a GP and I do believe in a healthy attitude to food, starting with families eating the same food all together. 99*
> *Louise, mum to Ella, 5 years, Eliza, 3 years, Molly, 22 months and Alice, 4 months*

A balanced diet for a seven to nine-month-old baby

Up until now, your baby may just have been getting used to having other foods as well as milk, but at this age she needs the nutrients that solids provide. The nutrient stores she was born with are no longer sufficient to support all her needs for growth and development, so what you give her to eat becomes more important. Fruits and vegetables are still necessary, but she now needs other foods too to meet her requirements.

Each day try to give your baby:

- two to three servings of starchy foods (e.g. baby rice, porridge, pasta, potato) – as a rough guide, about one-third of each meal should be starchy foods
- one serving of meat, fish, pulses (e.g. lentils) or well-cooked egg
- two to three servings of fruit and vegetables
- 500–600ml of formula or about three or four breastfeeds.

These guidelines apply whether your baby is having purées, mashed meals, finger foods or a mixture.

Iron

Providing an adequate iron intake can be particularly difficult at this age. As many as 20% of eight-month-old babies are anaemic, according to one study carried out in South West England. The likelihood of anaemia was found to be slightly higher among those who were breastfed (32%) than in those on formula (20%). This doesn't mean that formula milk is better for babies at this age; breast milk offers many advantages. But it does suggest that breastfeeding mothers shouldn't be complacent and think their milk will provide all the nutrients their baby needs. Babies of this age need solid foods as well.

The researchers in this study also found out that the babies with higher fibre and calcium intakes were at greater risk of iron deficiency. This is because both high-fibre foods and calcium reduce the absorption of iron in the intestines. They also found that those with lower protein intakes were at greater risk. The main problem seemed to be that those with the highest intakes of milk (more than six breastfeeds or more than 600ml of formula per day) weren't getting enough iron from solids. They were having 20% to 30% less solids than babies who had less milk, and this meant they were missing out on important sources of iron such as commercial baby foods, fortified breakfast cereals, vegetables, meat and fish.

> TIP Don't give your baby more than 600ml of formula or more than six breastfeeds a day. Otherwise she might be too full to eat all the solids she needs, which means she could miss out on essential nutrients.

Fish

We know that oily fish, such as salmon and mackerel, supply omega 3 fatty acids, which are important for your baby's brain and eye development (see p18). However, if that isn't reason enough to start giving fish to your baby now, then you might be interested in research carried out in Sweden, which found that fish can also reduce the risks of eczema and other allergic conditions. These studies, and others carried out in Australia and Norway, found that it's not just oily fish that offers this protection; white fish seems to have the same effect. Since offering your baby fish is such an easy thing to do, it makes sense to include fish dishes when you can.

> 66 *I've given them all fish from about six or seven months old, things like tuna with mashed potato. At the moment, they love baked salmon with noodles and sweetcorn – they had it at a noodle bar and thought it was great, so now I recreate it at home. They like fish fingers too and other fish in breadcrumbs, also prawns and tuna. I always do a quick check for bones, but I buy fillets and I've never found any bones yet. 99*
> *Máiréad, mum to Ailish, 6 years, Niall, 4 years and Orla, 1 year*

Fruit and vegetables

Most children don't eat enough fruit and vegetables, and it can be very difficult to get them started if they're not used to them. So it's a good idea to do everything possible to get your baby to accept these healthy foods while you can.

Research carried out in Philadelphia in the USA, with four to nine-month-old babies, found that the more often you give a baby fruit and vegetables, the more likely they are to eat them and enjoy them. Babies who were given pear every day for a week were found to increase their intake and show less 'negative faces' when they were given it. Likewise, babies given green beans were found to increase their intake after being given them repeatedly. It was also found that giving babies a variety of other vegetables resulted in them eating more green beans. So a baby's liking for a particular vegetable isn't just based on whether or not they've had it before, but on how often they eat vegetables generally. The American study also found that giving vegetables as snacks, as well as at meal times, increased babies' liking for them even more.

> TIP Give your baby as many different fruits and vegetables as possible. This way she'll get a range of nutrients and phytochemicals. Also, if she becomes fussy in the future and refuses a few, she should still be getting a reasonable intake.

Meals for your seven to nine-month-old

It's a good idea to start organising meal times for about the same time every day to get your baby into the habit of eating meals. Your baby will get used to this, and when she knows what to expect, she will be more likely to eat her meals happily.

Try to remember that your job is to provide the right foods for your baby; whether or not they are eaten is up to her. This means providing three nutritious meals and one or two healthy snacks each day. Then letting your baby eat as much of them as she likes.

As you start thinking more about your baby's nutrient intake, try not to get too anxious about what she actually eats. This sounds simple, but it can be difficult to put into practice. When you see a baby enjoying her food, it can reinforce feelings that she's healthy and doing well and that you're a good parent. There is a lot of emotion tied up in feeding babies and children, but if you can get used to this idea – of 'offering' food rather than 'getting it in' to your baby – you will avoid a lot of food battles later on.

If you started weaning by giving completely smooth purées, it's important to move on to lumpier foods now (see p38). You can either make the transition slowly by using a hand blender and simply stopping before the food is really smooth, or you can start mashing meals with a potato masher or a fork. If you delay starting your baby on lumpier food and leave it until later, it will only become more difficult. If you've been giving your baby stage 1 jars, you might find the transition to courser stage 2 meals difficult, but by giving a combination of homemade meals as well as jars, or by introducing more finger foods, it can be made easier.

At this stage, it's good for babies to have the opportunity to have finger foods as often as possible. If you can, try to provide some kind of finger food at each meal, as well as for snacks. If this isn't possible, it is still important to make sure they are included every day.

Are puddings a good idea?

One school of thought says that it's better not to give babies pudding after every meal. As babies have an innate preference for sweet foods, some decide very early on that they'd rather have pudding than vegetables and other foods. If pudding is fresh fruit it's not a big problem, but it's good to get babies eating and enjoying a varied diet that includes vegetables. This is one of those things that is really up to you. The theory makes sense, but plenty of babies have both savoury and sweet foods for lunch and dinner and enjoy them both.

TIP If your baby coughs or gags when she's eating, try to stay calm. It's quite common, so try not to overreact by jumping up to slap her back immediately. This will put her off and make her panicky about lumps. A bit of gagging is unlikely to worry your baby unless she sees you looking anxious. See p32 for more about choking.

Introducing cutlery

Between seven and nine months, babies are ready to start trying to feed themselves with a spoon. So whether you've been doing BLW or you've been giving purées, now is a good time to give your baby a spoon. At first, very little will make it to her mouth, but your baby will only learn by trying, so let her have a go. You can help her along by using a spoon yourself or by loading her spoon and letting her get it to her mouth herself.

As your baby tries to feed herself more, you'll find meal times can be very messy. Try to resist the temptation to wipe your baby's mouth or hands until she's finished. Instead, let her get stuck in and enjoy experimenting.

Breakfast

Breakfast is believed by many to be the most important meal of the day, but it is also the one that is most often skipped, even by babies. While adults often blame a lack of time or worries about their weight, babies have other excuses. A common reason for babies turning up their noses at breakfast is that they're full. Most have a big breastfeed or a whole bottle of milk in the morning and this is enough to fill them up. So if your baby doesn't seem keen on breakfast, make sure you're not giving more milk than is needed. If she finishes a bottle then cries for more, give her breakfast instead of any extra. Alternatively, if you usually offer breakfast straight after the milk feed, try just waiting a little while until she's not so full.

School children who eat breakfast have been shown to behave better, to be more alert in class and to achieve better marks in a variety of tests. Breakfast-eaters of all ages are also less likely to be overweight than breakfast skippers. For babies and toddlers, fortified breakfast cereals are also an important source of iron and B vitamins.

Even if mornings are very busy in your house, as you rush to get to work or prepare older children for school, try to make time for your baby to eat. A bowl of breakfast cereal doesn't take long, but provides a good start to the day (see p87 for advice on choosing the best cereal). If there really isn't time for breakfast first thing, then maybe she could have some after the rush is over, or, if she's going to nursery, once she gets there.

Quick breakfast foods

- Weetabix or similar own-brand cereals
- Instant hot oat cereal (e.g. Ready Brek)
- Regular porridge made with oats and milk
- Baby breakfasts containing fruit and cereals with extra iron and vitamins
- Shreddies or similar own-brand cereals
- Wholemeal toast

These starchy breakfast cereals can be given with full-fat cows' milk or infant formula. It's also good to offer some fruit, such as banana, ripe pear or strawberries, either mashed or as finger food.

Most breakfast cereals such as porridge or Weetabix mixed with milk are too runny for babies to feed to themselves at this age. If you don't want to spoon-feed your baby, or if she's decided you're not allowed to, then you need to be a bit more inventive. You can try giving cereal such as Weetabix or Shreddies (or the own-brand equivalent) with just a tiny amount of milk – not so much as to make them too soggy to pick up, but enough to prevent them being dry. Soon your baby will master a spoon and this won't be necessary.

Breakfast for days when there's a bit more time

- Oaty pancakes (see recipe, p152)
- Scrambled eggs
- Oats mixed with grated apple and milk
- French toast

These breakfasts make a nice weekend treat for all the family, especially if you eat them with fresh fruit and yogurt. They're also good for babies who don't like breakfast cereals.

Lunch and dinner

The type of food you give your baby for lunch and dinner can be fairly interchangeable at this stage. If you usually eat a sandwich at lunchtime and something hot in the evening, at a time that suits your baby, then that is ideal and you can eat together. She can have finger foods in the middle of the day, and foods from your meal later on.

However, if you usually eat later than your baby in the evening, then perhaps you can share lunch together. If you're having a thick soup, she could have some of it mashed, or you could give her some of the lumps.

Or, you might decide to give her the food that you ate the evening before. Although you're not eating the same food at the same time, it works quite well for many families and it helps your baby get used to eating family foods. Leftover pasta can make a good lunch for a baby. It has the advantage over bread of containing much less salt and you can mix it with a variety of other foods. Different ways of doing things may work on different days, depending on what you're doing and what you're eating yourself.

Pasta lunches

For an easy lunch, leftover pasta can be mixed with:

- puréed vegetables
- avocado, cottage cheese and peas
- houmous and yogurt
- mashed sardines (canned in tomato sauce), mixed with natural yogurt
- cheddar cheese and mashed cauliflower
- lemony lentil dip (see p155)
- mackerel pâté (see p157) with extra yogurt.

Whereas younger babies generally lack the skills to feed themselves enough to meet their nutritional needs, as they become more able, this becomes easier. When your baby can manage to feed herself fairly well, you can provide whole meals as finger foods. Some parents who like the idea of BLW, but find it doesn't always work, give their baby pieces of food, and if they can't manage, they put the pieces in a bowl and whiz them up with the blender. It may be easier to give part of the meal mushed up and part of it as finger foods.

Finger foods to try

- Toast soldiers or pitta bread strips
- Cubes or sticks of hard cheese, such as cheddar and edam
- Cooked vegetables, such as green beans, carrots, and sweet potato
- Rice cakes
- Apple (not all babies can manage this yet)
- Cooked pasta shapes
- Sticks of raw cucumber
- Thick slices of avocado
- Fruit such as pears and peaches, whole or quartered (if you offer a whole peach, make sure you take away the stone when your baby reaches it)
- Pieces of meat, chicken or fish

How to prepare meat

You can serve your baby meat by cutting it into strips, like the vegetables. Make it easier by giving her strips that are big enough to stick out of the end of her fist. Pieces about 5cm long should be about right. Sometimes bigger pieces are easier, so you could also try chicken legs or even chops, as these are both a good shape for grasping.

To avoid the risk of choking, it is best to remove any skin and visible fat or gristle and any small splinter bones. With red meat such as beef, it's best to cut across the fibres, then it's easier for your baby to pull the meat apart to eat it. As well as offering meals with meat, remember to offer a variety of other protein foods, including meals made with fish, and vegetarian meals.

Salmon kedgeree

½ tablespoon olive oil
½ small onion (peeled and chopped)
2–3 mushrooms (chopped)
75g dried basmati rice
Juice and zest of ¼ lemon
1 level teaspoon dried parsley
Water
1 salmon fillet
1–2 heaped tablespoons frozen peas

Preparation time: 30 minutes
Pans: 1
Storage: Suitable for freezing; keeps in the fridge for up to 24 hours.
Servings: Makes 1 adult portion or 4–5 baby portions. The recipe is suitable for the whole family, so you can simply increase the quantities as needed.

- Heat the olive oil in a pan and sauté the onion and mushroom until soft. Add the rice, parsley, lemon juice and zest and enough water to cover these ingredients. Bring to the boil and simmer.
- Meanwhile, cut the salmon into cubes. As you do this, you will be able to check that there are no bones in the fish.
- When the rice is nearly cooked add the salmon and peas, turn up the heat and cook until the salmon has changed colour and everything is hot. Add more water if necessary.

Your baby can eat it as it is, or you can use a hand blender to mush it slightly.

Tomato medley

200g broccoli
200g cauliflower
1 tin chopped tomatoes (400g)
1 tablespoon mixed herbs
400g potatoes
2 teaspoons margarine

Preparation time: 40 minutes
Pans: 2
Storage: Suitable for freezing; keeps in the fridge for up to 24 hours.
Servings: Makes 10 baby portions.

- Peel the potatoes and cut into chunks. Place them in a pan with just enough water to cover them.
- Put the lid on and bring to the boil, then turn down the heat and simmer for about 20 minutes or until tender.
- Meanwhile, chop the broccoli and cauliflower into small florets and place in a pan with 100ml of water. Cover and bring to the boil, then simmer for 10 minutes.
- Add the tomatoes and herbs and simmer for 10 minutes more. Then add the drained potatoes and the margarine and mash all the ingredients together.

Tips

- This recipe is great for iron. As well as containing iron-rich vegetables, it includes vitamin C and citric acid, which increase the absorption of iron.
- You can add cheese or leftover chicken to the recipe.

Carrot and coriander mash

1 tablespoon olive oil
1 onion (peeled and finely chopped)
400g carrots
400g potatoes
125g dried red lentils (washed)
1 teaspoon coriander

Preparation time: 30 minutes
Pans: 1
Storage: Suitable for freezing; keeps in the fridge for up to 24 hours.
Servings: Makes 6–8 baby portions.

- Heat the oil in a frying pan. Add the onion and sauté until transparent and soft. Add the coriander, lentils and three cups of water. Bring to the boil and boil rapidly for 15 minutes.
- While this is boiling, peel the potatoes and carrots and cut them into small pieces.
- After 15 minutes, add the potatoes and carrots to the lentil mixture. Cover the pan and simmer until soft. Mash with a potato masher and divide into portions.

Cheesy leek and potato pie

1 tablespoon olive oil
1–2 leeks (depending on size)
6 broccoli florets (finely chopped)
2 large potatoes (peeled and chopped)
1 teaspoon mixed herbs
50g cheddar cheese (grated)
50ml milk

Preparation time: 30 minutes

Pans: 2

Storage: Suitable for freezing; keeps in the fridge for up to 24 hours.

Servings: Makes enough for two adults and a baby or about 10 baby portions.

- Peel and chop the potatoes, place them in a pan covered with water and bring to the boil. Simmer until soft.
- Meanwhile, cut the leek lengthways into thin strips then chop.
- Heat the oil in a pan. Sauté the leek until soft but not browned (about five minutes) then add the chopped broccoli, 50ml of water and herbs, cover and cook until soft. If the vegetables start to brown or stick to the bottom of the pan add more water.
- When the leek and broccoli are cooked, you can purée them slightly with a blender or leave them as they are.
- Then add the drained potatoes, cheese and milk and mash all the ingredients together.
- If you want a crispy top, you can put it into a serving dish and brown it under the grill for a few minutes.

Tips

- The leek won't break up when you mash it, so it needs to be finely chopped
- It goes nicely with a tomato salad for lunch
- For a main meal, you could eat it with grilled fish or chicken and roast vegetables
- It's great for babies to feed themselves as it won't fall off the spoon – even if you want it to!

Snacks

As your baby gets older and more active, she will start to need snacks as well as meals. Most babies this age will have a snack and a drink of water mid-morning and another snack mid-afternoon.

Biscuits and rusks are an easy option, but they don't provide the nutrients your baby needs. If you start to give snacks like this, it will be very hard to encourage healthier eating habits later.

Your baby doesn't know that when most people talk about 'snack foods' they're thinking of biscuits or crisps, rather than cold potatoes or rice cakes, and long may this innocence last. Your baby will become more streetwise soon enough and she may well start demanding crisps or sweets in the future, but you can think about that later. For now, she doesn't know any different, so make snacks as healthy as possible. Rather than providing treats, you can give some of the foods that she might miss out on at meal times.

Suitable snacks

- Toast, pitta or chapatti fingers
- Pieces of chopped fruit
- Cooked vegetable sticks
- Small cubes or sticks of cheese
- Cold boiled or roast potatoes
- Rice cakes
- Breadsticks
- Baked toast fingers (see p121)
- Scone fingers (see below)

Scone fingers

50g margarine
225g self-raising flour
5ml baking powder
100ml milk
Extra flour for dusting

Preparation time: 30 minutes (including 10 minutes baking time)
Pans: 2 baking trays
Storage: Store in an airtight container for a few days. Also suitable for freezing.
Servings: Makes 32 fingers.

- Preheat the oven to 230°C/450°F/gas mark 8.
- Rub the margarine into the flour and baking powder. Blend in the milk until you have a soft dough.
- Turn the dough out onto a lightly floured surface and knead lightly.
- Divide the mixture in half, then half again and so on to make eight, then 16, and then 32 pieces.

- Roll each of these with your hands to make a stick, which is about the thickness of your little finger and 7–8cm long.
- Place on a greased baking tray and bake for 5–10 minutes.

Tips

- Add dried fruit for a change, such as 50g of raisins or chopped apricots
- If you want to make a richer scone, add an egg to the mixture
- To make a savoury version, add 75g of grated cheese

Drinks

Your baby's main drink should still be breast milk or formula until she reaches 12 months. If you're breastfeeding, three to four feeds a day should be enough. If your baby is having formula, then 500–600ml a day is recommended. More than this can fill up your baby and result in a poor appetite and intake of solids.

It is fine to use cows' milk when you're preparing meals, such as mashed potatoes, but it is still not suitable as a main drink. If you're thinking about switching to anything other than a formula based on cows' milk, for example a soya-based formula, talk to your health visitor.

Some babies are still waking up in the night for a feed at this age, but healthy babies who were born at full term shouldn't need to. Unfortunately, it can be a hard habit to break, but if your baby is gaining weight then maybe you just need to get a bit stricter. It will help if you make sure that during the day she gets all the solids and milk she needs. Then you can try offering only water in the night to try to break the night-time pattern.

> TIP Now that your baby is having more solids, she needs to drink more fluids. Water is the best drink to offer and babies should have a cup available throughout the day. It is particularly important to offer her water during each meal and snack, as between times it may be forgotten.

If your baby isn't drinking much water, it may be tempting to give her something else, but bear in mind that squash, flavoured milk, fruit juice and other fruit drinks contain natural sugars and acids. If you want to give her these drinks, then they should be diluted (one part juice to 10 parts water). Even when they are diluted, they can still contribute to tooth decay, so they should only be given at meal times. Parents sometimes decide to give sweetened drinks just for a short while, until their baby gets used to drinking from a cup and having something other than milk. However, babies really do develop a sweet tooth at an early age. Research investigating the level of sweetness preferred by two-year-olds found that those given sweetened drinks as babies preferred more sugary drinks.

What to expect in your baby's nappy

By the time your baby is seven months old, her poo should be looking quite different to how it looked before you started weaning. If it still looks like the poo of an exclusively breastfed or bottle-fed baby, it may mean she isn't having enough solids.

If your baby is having only finger foods, it can be difficult to tell how much she's really eating. However, if her poo is looking more like adult poo, you know she's really eating.

Stage 2 meal plan

The meal plan below is here to give you an idea of the types of meals you can give your baby to make sure she gets all her required nutrients. It has been specifically designed to meet a seven to nine-month-old baby's requirements for energy, protein, potassium, calcium, magnesium, phosphorus, iron, copper, zinc, chloride, selenium, iodine, thiamin, riboflavin, niacin, folic acid and vitamins A, B6, B12, C, D and E. Also, each day's menu contains less than 1g of salt, which is the maximum amount a baby this age should have in a day.

You don't have to follow it exactly, but when you're planning what to give your baby it should give you some ideas.

You might notice that the meal plan includes:

- specially prepared baby meals, such as tomato medley (see p138)

- family meals such as Sunday roast with lamb. A baby eating this shouldn't have the same gravy as everyone else as it is likely to be too salty. Your baby could eat a meal like this with her hands, or if you wanted to mush the meal you could add some of the water from cooking the vegetables
- simple meals made from leftover pasta, or mashed potatoes with tinned fish
- both finger foods and puréed or mashed foods at most meals. Some foods, such as broccoli and carrots, could be eaten with fingers or mashed, depending on your baby
- convenience foods, but only those suitable for babies, such as fortified breakfast cereals and the odd jar of baby dessert.

Day	Breakfast	Snack	Lunch	Snack	Dinner
1	Weetabix with milk Half a banana	Plain rice cakes	Carrot and coriander mash (see p139) Half a pear	Milk feed Half a slice of toast with houmous	Mashed sardines in tomato sauce mixed with pasta Broccoli spears (as finger food) Strawberries and natural yogurt
2	Hot oat cereal (e.g. Ready Brek) with milk Half a pear	Steamed green beans (cold)	Lamb, roast potatoes, carrot and cauliflower Half a banana with custard	Milk feed Plain rice cakes	Cheesy leek and potato pie (see p139) Halved cherry tomatoes
3	Baby porridge with milk	Roast potato (cold)	Roast sweet potato, carrot and parsnip with houmous Apple purée with natural yogurt	Milk feed Mini breadsticks and cubes of cheddar	Pasta mixed with chicken, peas, avocado and yogurt Jar of baby rice pudding

4	Weetabix with milk Pieces of melon	Plain rice cakes with almond butter	Tomato medley (see p138) Cubes or grated cheese Half a peach	Milk feed Two scone fingers (see p141)	Scrambled egg, toast fingers and cherry tomatoes Pear purée (see p112)
5	Hot oat cereal with milk Slices of mango	Half a banana	Tuna with mashed potato Green beans Yogurt and apple purée	Milk feed Two toast fingers	Spaghetti bolognaise Half a peach
6	Baby porridge with milk Half a pear	Mini breadsticks and cubes of cheese	Carrot and coriander mash (see p139) Melon and kiwi	Milk feed Plain rice cake with peanut butter	Chicken and baked sweet potato Broccoli spears Jar of fruity rice pudding
7	Fingers of cheese omelette and toast Pieces of tomato	Two cheese scone fingers (see p141)	Salmon kedgeree (see p137) Carrot sticks Jar of fruity yogurt	Milk feed Half a banana	Cottage pie (see p156) Slices of mango

You might also notice that it doesn't include any biscuits, rusks or other snack foods with added flavouring. Instead, snacks consist of fruit, vegetables, or plain unsweetened foods such as breadsticks and rice cakes. Bearing these features in mind will help you to plan your baby's meals and snacks.

In addition to these meals and snacks, babies should have a breastfeed or a bottle of formula when they wake and another before bed. These two feeds, along with a third, usually mid-afternoon, should provide your baby with 500–600ml of milk per day, which is all she needs. Your baby will also need a cup of water with each meal and snack.

8

Stage 3:
nine to 12 months

By the time your baby is 12 months old, she should be fitting in with family meal times and eating a varied diet. So as she approaches her first birthday, it's time to think about establishing really good eating habits with regular meals and healthy snacks.

Growing in independence

Once babies are a year old, they often start to exert their independence at the table and become fussier about what they eat. So take the opportunity now to introduce a wide variety of foods while she may be more willing to try new things. This includes offering her dishes with a bit more flavour, such as mild curries, and with different textures, like couscous or raw carrot and apple.

Now is also the time when handling food, experimenting and self-feeding really takes off, and this should be encouraged. Inevitably meal times will be messy, but it is a stage your baby has to go through, so just try to enjoy her newfound skills.

Most babies are now sitting up confidently and trying to feed themselves more. It's best if your baby is in a highchair for meals rather than on your lap, as this will give her a greater sense of independence and make it easier for her to feed herself. In any case, self-feeding with hands should become more efficient at this age, as a baby's pincer grip enables her to pick up small pieces of food more easily. As well as encouraging your baby to pick food up with her hands, you should give her a spoon so she can get used to feeding herself runny foods too. Help her if you feel she needs it, but try to do this less and less.

> 66 *Rosa is fascinated by food and does that little shake of the head before the spoon hits her lips, like she can't get it fast enough. There's nothing she won't eat and she's desperate to feed herself. She's the complete opposite to George, who's never had any interest in food and can't be bothered feeding himself even now. My mum says he's just an exaggerated version of what I was like. My conclusion is it's just innate, so don't bother fighting it.* 99
> **Saroop, mum to George, 2 years and Rosa, 11 months**

As your baby's character develops and she becomes more skilled, you may find that she doesn't want to be spoon-fed by you anymore. You might see this as a nuisance to start with, as she probably can't feed herself very efficiently, but really it's a positive step towards independence at meal times and should be welcomed.

> TIP Give your baby a spoon and fork and encourage her to feed herself as much as possible. Whether you started with baby-led weaning (BLW) or purées, your baby should now be given the opportunity to feed herself with her hands and with cutlery.

Some babies might not be very interested in feeding themselves, but others love it. By smearing mashed potato or bashing a piece of broccoli on the table, your baby will have the chance to find out more about it. A baby may well want to play with a new food to familiarise herself with it, before deciding to taste it. If she doesn't have the opportunity to do so, she might not feel confident enough to try to eat it. So it's best to minimise mess as best you can, but allow your baby to explore her food as much as possible.

Joining in meal times

Between about nine and 12 months, babies become more aware of what other people are eating and meal times will become much more of a social occasion. If you can include your baby in family meals whenever possible, you'll certainly start to see the benefits: she'll be noticing what you eat and how you use cutlery and may start to copy you.

She'll also be getting used to eating the foods that you eat, which will make life much easier for you in the future. By sharing in family meals, your baby will also be less likely to grow up as a fussy eater. You can help to make meal times as relaxed and enjoyable as possible by chatting with your baby and letting her see how you eat.

> 66 *I love eating together and it means that Oscar has learned very quickly what to do. He sits in his highchair beside us and has his own food, but he likes to join in too, so if we're having something like chicken, I'll give him some, or he'll have slices of carrot or apple. From about 10 months, he started grabbing for food and spoons. He watches everyone and sees what we're doing and copies. He's become quite good using a spoon already.* 99
> **Gilda, mum to Natalia, 10 years, Ilaria, 7 years and Oscar, 12 months**

Bigger appetites

Most babies start to get on the move now, whether they're rolling, crawling, bum shuffling or walking. All this activity uses up energy and you may notice an increase in appetite. Being guided by your baby's appetite is crucial, and if she's feeding herself more, it should be easier to see when she loses interest and has had enough.

Try to avoid using meal-time games to encourage her to eat up. She may enjoy it, but she should be eating because she's hungry and wants to eat, not so that you'll play with her. Likewise, as your baby's understanding develops, she'll learn the word 'no', and if you use it every time she throws food, it can turn into a game too, so it's best just to ignore it. During a meal, if she starts smearing food all over the tray, or dropping it off the edge of the highchair for you to fetch, it probably means she's had enough.

How to minimise meal-time mess

- Get a bib with sleeves or roll up clothes past the elbow
- Use a cup with a lid
- Put food in a bowl rather than on a plate
- Cover the floor with a mat, old towel or newspaper
- Don't offer too many foods at the same time (two or three are enough)
- Don't encourage things such as food throwing by laughing
- End the meal when eating stops and playing escalates
- Invest in a mini hoover!

A balanced diet for a nine to 12-month-old baby

Babies should now be eating three good meals a day. Most also need two snacks as well.

Each day, try to offer your baby:

- three or four servings of starchy foods (e.g. bread, rice and potato)
- three or four servings of fruit and vegetables – varieties rich in vitamin C, such as oranges, strawberries and broccoli, will help with iron absorption, so it is good to give these at meal times
- two servings of meat, fish, eggs, lentils or other pulses
- about three or four breastfeeds a day or 500–600ml of formula. Some of this can be taken with food or substituted with other dairy foods.

Although milk is still an important source of calcium and vitamins A, D and B12, your baby doesn't need more than the recommended amount. Otherwise she could miss out on other foods and nutrients. If she has foods made from milk, such as cheese, yogurt or fromage frais, she doesn't need as much milk to drink. You should also count milk on breakfast cereal when you're working out how much she's having every day. Remember that while low-fat dairy foods are good for adults, your baby should still be having full-fat varieties.

Fat is an important source of calories for babies, but it is important to keep a balanced approach. You don't want your baby to get used to having her bread with a thick layer of margarine on it, or her vegetables covered in melted butter. Whereas dairy foods provide protein, vitamins and minerals, butter and margarine are mainly fat. It's better for babies to get used to having their vegetables without any fat, and to have only a thin covering of spread on their bread. Oily fish and foods such as avocado and nut butters are much better sources of fat. These provide polyunsaturated and monounsaturated fatty acids, which are healthier than the saturated fat found in foods such as butter and processed meat products.

> 66 *Ethan will eat anything. My nanny made him puréed vegetables to start with, but when we saw my mum, she always gave him whatever we were eating, if it wasn't spicy. I suppose it's how she fed us as babies. He likes my mum's cooking now, especially when she gives him bits of paratha.* 99
> **Angie, mum to Ethan, 11 months**

When you're planning meals, bear in mind the old 'meat and two veg' idea. Lunch and dinner should include a protein food, a starchy food, and vegetables. If your baby doesn't have a portion of meat or fish every day, try to provide two portions of other protein foods instead, including eggs, lentils and pulses, such as chickpeas.

Babies, like the rest of us, don't need to have meat every day, and health experts, including those at the WCRF, believe a more vegetarian-style diet could be beneficial for everyone. So introducing your baby to different types of beans and pulses will create some good habits to see her through to adulthood. Houmous, made from chickpeas, is very popular with babies. You could also try making pasta sauce with lentils, or adding butter beans or haricot beans to a stew or casserole. If your baby is having a completely vegetarian diet, then you can find out more about ensuring all her nutrient needs are met in Chapter 14.

Meals for your nine to 12-month-old

Your baby should be moving away from puréed or mashed foods now and towards chopped meals or meals made up of whole pieces of food. You shouldn't need to use a blender for entire meals any more, although you might find it useful for dips, especially if your baby prefers to feed herself.

You should be able to give your baby the same food that the rest of the family is having now. Hopefully this will have a positive influence on her diet, giving her the opportunity to enjoy a variety of healthy and freshly cooked foods, rather than tucking into takeaways or sausage and chips.

It will do the whole family good to avoid having processed foods such as sausages and pies too often, and it is better for your baby if she never gets into the habit of having foods like this.

> TIP There is very little your baby can't eat at this age, but the main thing you need to be careful about when giving her family meals is avoiding too much salt.
>
> If you want salt on your own food, then you could add it once it's ready, rather than during cooking. It's also important to be aware of other high-salt ingredients, such as stock cubes (see p24).

Breakfast

The breakfast foods suggested for seven to nine-month-old babies are still great for babies as they approach 12 months (see p134). A fortified cereal is a good way to start the day, but if your baby wants to feed herself, or if you want to try other foods for a bit of variety, then you could try dishes that include egg.

Scrambled eggs with toast, or French toast, (also known as eggy bread) are worth a try. For both these dishes, you simply beat the egg in a bowl and heat up a frying pan containing a little margarine. Then, either pour in the egg and stir (for scrambled eggs) or soak the bread in the egg before frying (for French toast). Alternatively you can make pancakes.

This is a good way of giving your baby eggs without the food tasting so 'eggy', which may put off some babies. These dishes can be served with fruit or vegetables, such as chopped cherry tomatoes or strawberries and other berries.

Oaty pancakes

100g plain flour
100g oats
1 teaspoon baking powder
2 eggs
250ml whole milk
1 tablespoon vegetable oil plus extra for frying

Preparation time: 25–30 minutes
Pans: 1 plus a mixing bowl
Storage: Suitable for freezing: place in an airtight container, separated by sheets of greaseproof paper or baking parchment.
Servings: Makes 22 pancakes.

- Put the oats, flour and baking powder into a bowl and make a well in the centre.
- Crack the eggs into it and pour in the milk and oil, then beat either with a fork or a wire whisk.
- Next, heat some oil in a frying pan until sizzling, then drop in a tablespoonful of the mixture. The mixture will spread out slightly and you should be able to make about four or five pancakes like this at the same time.
- When you can see the edges are cooked and the top has a few bubbles, turn it over with a spatula or fish slice and cook the other side. Each side takes one or two minutes to cook.

Tips

- You can add a few raisins or some mashed banana for a change
- Add some grated cheese for a savoury version
- When you've cooked a batch, you can keep them warm in the oven while you cook more, then everyone can eat together
- Serve with fruit compote or purée
- To reheat pancakes that have been frozen, place under the grill for a few minutes

Lunch and dinner

The recipes we've included for main meals in this chapter are for the *whole* family, as the aim is for everyone to eat together whenever possible. Of course this doesn't always work out, and some days you might need to just throw a quick meal together for your baby. You'll find plenty of easy meal ideas in this chapter and in the meal plan at the end of the chapter.

> TIP Pasta is easy to cook, but try not to give it to your baby every day. Give other starchy foods such as potatoes, rice and couscous too.

When you're planning meals, it might be worth thinking about how easy they are for self-feeding. Dishes such as shepherd's pie are a favourite in many households, and because the mixture of potato and mince sticks to a spoon fairly well, your baby will be able to feed herself more easily. Meals including rice and peas might be more difficult, but it all depends on your baby and how determined she is. As she learns to cope with larger chunks of food, you might find she struggles with certain dishes, such as pieces of meat, and if this is the case just cut things up a bit more for her.

> TIP Don't give your baby too much bread or toast. Each slice contains 0.5g of salt, so if she has a slice for breakfast and another for lunch, she's likely to go over the daily maximum for her age (1g salt per day).

Now is the time to really add variety to your baby's diet. Offer her a wide range from each of the food groups. Include different starchy foods with each meal and give her as many different-coloured fruit and vegetables as possible. Also, try to mix and match between different protein foods such as meat, fish and the alternatives, like lentils (mentioned above).

Dips and spreads

As babies become better at eating with their hands, and even start refusing to be spoon-fed, finger foods with a spread or dip can be invaluable. With a bit of planning, it's possible for babies to get all the nutrients they need from meals like this. These types of meals may also encourage those who are less keen on feeding themselves.

Foods for dipping

- Toast fingers or strips of pitta bread
- Rice cakes
- Carrot and cucumber sticks
- Breadsticks
- Cooked vegetable sticks (see p119)
- Roast vegetables (see p120)
- Oven chips
- Pieces of meat, chicken and fish
- Apple wedges

Dips

- Houmous
- Lentil dhal
- Cheese sauce
- Vegetable purée
- Guacamole
- Lemony lentil dip (see opposite page)

Spreads

- Tinned sardine mashed with cream cheese or ricotta cheese
- Tinned salmon ('no added salt', otherwise it's very salty) mashed with cream cheese or ricotta and lemon juice
- Nut butters, such as peanut, almond or cashew
- Mashed avocado and houmous
- Mackerel pâté (see p157)

Most of these spreads can be turned into dips by mixing them with some natural yogurt. If you make a dip too runny, you might find more of it ends up on your baby or her highchair than in her mouth, but if it's too thick, your baby won't be able to scoop it up. By experimenting you'll be able to work out what suits your baby. You can also make dips with leftover bolognaise or other pasta sauce. This is particularly good for babies who won't eat these foods otherwise.

Lemony lentil dip

150g dried red lentils
750ml cold water
150g carrots
1 tablespoon olive oil
1 small onion (finely chopped)
1 inch piece of fresh ginger (peeled and grated)
1 clove of garlic (peeled and crushed)
½ teaspoon turmeric
½ teaspoon coriander
Juice and zest of ½ lemon
50g cream cheese

Preparation time: 25 minutes
Pans: 2
Storage: Suitable for freezing; keeps in the fridge for up to 24 hours.
Servings: Makes about 5 adult portions or 12–18 baby portions.

- Place the lentils and water in a pan, bring to the boil and boil rapidly for 10 minutes. Meanwhile, peel and dice the carrots into small pieces. Then add the carrots to the lentils, cover and simmer for 10–15 minutes until they are soft.
- While this is cooking, heat the oil in another pan and gently fry the onion, ginger and garlic for five minutes. Add the spices and lemon zest and cook for two minutes more, stirring all the time.
- When the carrots are cooked, drain any excess liquid.
- Add the onion mixture and lemon juice, and blend the mixture in a liquidiser or with a hand-held blender.
- Stir in the cream cheese, then put the mixture into a bowl and put it in the fridge to set slightly.

Tips

- If you leave it in the fridge for about six hours it will set and be more suitable for spreading on toast
- As well as serving this with vegetables and pitta strips, you can mix it with leftover pasta for an easy lunch or dinner
- If your baby can't have dairy foods, just leave out the cream cheese and the dip will still taste great

Cottage pie

1 onion (finely chopped)
1 tablespoon olive oil
1–2 cloves garlic (crushed)
450g lean minced beef
2 tablespoon mixed herbs
1 low-salt stock cube (optional)
1 tin chopped tomatoes (400g)
1 tablespoon tomato purée
750g potatoes
100ml milk
2 teaspoons butter or margarine

Preparation time: 1 hour (including 20–30 minutes in the oven)
Pans: 2 plus an oven dish
Storage: Suitable for freezing; keeps in the fridge for up to 24 hours.
Servings: Makes enough for a family of four to six.

- Preheat the oven to 200°C/400°F/gas mark 6.
- Peel and chop the potatoes and cover with water. Then bring to the boil and simmer until soft.
- Meanwhile, heat the oil in a pan and sauté the onions, garlic and herbs for a few minutes. Add the mince and cook until it is browned all over, breaking up any lumps with a spoon.
- Mix in the chopped tomatoes and purée (plus stock cube if you're using one), bring to the boil and simmer for about 15 minutes.
- Meanwhile, drain the potatoes. Add the margarine or butter, plus the milk, and mash until smooth. You can add some black pepper at this stage, but it is best not to add any salt.
- Put the minced beef mixture into an ovenproof dish, spoon the potato on top and put it in the oven for about 30 minutes until nicely browned.

Tips

- This basic recipe can be expanded by adding other vegetables when you're cooking the onions, including finely chopped red pepper, carrots or mushrooms
- You can use lamb instead of beef if you wish and make shepherd's pie
- Serve with steamed carrot sticks or broccoli

Mackerel pâté

1 tin mackerel in oil or brine (125g)
½ tin cannelloni beans (½ of 400g)
1–2 tablespoons natural yogurt (depending how thick you want it)
2 tablespoons tomato purée
2 tablespoons lemon juice
Black pepper

Preparation time: 10 minutes
Pans: None, just a large bowl
Storage: Suitable for freezing; keeps in the fridge for up to 24 hours.
Servings: Makes enough for two adults and a baby for lunch, or about 4–6 baby portions.

- Drain the mackerel and the beans and place them in a bowl.
- Add all the other ingredients and mash with a fork or whiz with a hand-held blender.

Quick tuna pasta

200g pasta shapes (uncooked weight)
1 tablespoon olive oil
1 onion (finely chopped)
1–2 cloves garlic (crushed)
3–4 mushrooms (chopped)
1 tin chopped tomatoes (400g)
1 tin tuna (185g)
1 tablespoon mixed herbs

Preparation time: 30 minutes
Pans: 2
Storage: Suitable for freezing, keeps in the fridge for up to 24 hours.
Servings: Two adults and a baby.

- Cook the pasta in a pan of boiling water (without salt) and drain.
- Meanwhile, heat the oil in a pan and sauté the onion, mushrooms and garlic for a few minutes until soft.
- Add the herbs, tomato and tuna and allow to simmer for at least five minutes.

Tips

- You can add a variety of vegetables to this basic recipe, including finely chopped red pepper, carrot and celery, grated courgette, chopped aubergine or broccoli. These should be cooked with the onion and mushrooms.
- If your baby struggles with lumps or picks out bits you could purée the sauce slightly before mixing it with the pasta.
- Instead of using tuna, add tinned mackerel or sardine for extra omega 3 fatty acids.
- To make a vegetarian version, add 75g of split red lentils and 150ml water when you add the tinned tomato, bring to the boil and simmer for 15–20 minutes.
- If your baby can't have gluten you can use special gluten-free pasta or have the sauce with rice or potato instead.

Snacks and drinks

Mid-morning and mid-afternoon snacks often make a welcome break in the day – a time when your baby can sit still for a minute. Lots of children eat crisps and sweets before their first birthday, especially those with older brothers and sisters, but it really is better to establish good eating habits now to minimise battles in the future. Try to offer sweet snacks, such as biscuits, only occasionally or not at all. It's also good to make sure that foods and drinks between meals are as tooth-friendly as possible.

Hopefully your baby is in the habit of drinking water between meals; if not, now is probably the best chance you'll get to wean her off any fruit drinks and switch to plain water. This might not be a simple thing to do, but as your baby gets older it certainly won't get any easier.

Good snacks

- Bananas
- Mini pots of chopped fruit, e.g. grapes, kiwi or apple
- Mini boxes of raisins
- Breadsticks
- Scone fingers (see p141)
- Cold cooked pasta
- Oaty pancakes (see p152)

Stage 3 meal plan

In addition to the meals and snacks in the meal plan, babies should have a breastfeed or a bottle of formula when they wake and another before bed. These two feeds, along with a third feed, usually mid-afternoon, should provide your baby with 500–600ml of milk per day, which is all she needs. Your baby will also need a cup of water with each meal and snack.

Get fishy

We've looked already at the benefits of fish for long-term health (see p18). As your baby's brain is still growing rapidly, it's good to give her one or two portions of fish, including some oily fish, every week. You can easily incorporate it into favourite dishes, such as pasta sauce, or put mashed sardine on toast or in a dip.

Day	Breakfast	Snack	Lunch	Snack	Dinner
1	Oaty pancakes (see p152) and fruit compote or purée	Raisins	Lemony lentil dip (see p155) with pitta bread strips and cooked vegetables (carrot sticks, green beans, baby corn) Fromage frais	Milk feed Two scone fingers (see p141)	Quick tuna pasta (see p157) Kiwi and strawberries
2	Weetabix with milk Half a banana	Rice cakes and dried apricots	Pasta bows with peas, grated cheese, avocado and cottage cheese Orange segments	Milk feed Breadsticks	Toast with mackerel pâté (see p157), cucumber sticks and tomato pieces Fresh peach with yogurt

Continued over page

Continued from overleaf

Day	Breakfast	Snack	Lunch	Snack	Dinner
3	Hot oat cereal with milk Raisins	Breadsticks and a slice of edam	Roast chicken, roast potato, cauliflower, carrots and peas Fruit salad	Milk feed Small pear	Omelette, toast and leftover vegetables from lunch Apple crumble and custard
4	Shreddies with milk Half a banana	Two plums	Pasta mixed with lemony lentil dip (see p155) and carrot and cucumber sticks Jar of baby fruit pudding	Milk feed Mini houmous and avocado sandwich	Cottage pie (see p156) and green beans
5	Scrambled eggs and toast fingers	Small pear	Carrot and coriander mash (see p139) and broccoli spears	Milk feed Oaty pancakes.	Grilled salmon, baked potato with margarine and mange tout Mixed berries and yogurt
6	Baby muesli with milk Strawberries	Small banana	Tuna and cream cheese sandwich and halved cherry tomatoes Fruit yogurt	Milk feed Rice cakes with almond butter	Lamb chop, mashed potato and roast vegetables (butternut squash, parsnips and courgette) Mango slices
7	Weetabix with milk Pieces of melon	Apple wedges	Crusty bread with houmous and leftover roast vegetables Jar of rice pudding	Milk feed Breadsticks and cheese cubes	Cheesy leek and potato pie (see p139–140) Pieces of chicken and tomato Small peach

This meal plan has been designed to ensure it meets a nine to 12-month-old baby's requirements for energy, protein, potassium, calcium, magnesium, phosphorus, iron, copper, zinc, chloride, selenium, iodine, thiamin, riboflavin, niacin, folic acid and vitamins A, B6, B12, C, D and E. Also, each day's menu contains less than 1g of salt, which is the maximum amount a baby this age should have.

Like the previous menu plan (see p144), it doesn't have to be followed exactly, but will hopefully give you some ideas about the types of foods that will make up a healthy diet for your baby.

9

Toddlers and beyond

As your baby turns into a toddler, you'll be noticing lots of changes. She'll be growing in confidence and developing a whole host of new skills. If she hasn't been joining in family meals yet, she'll certainly be ready to now. Most one-year-olds are babbling away and quite expressive, so meal times are likely to become a lot more interactive.

You are likely to notice that between about 12 and 15 months your baby's appetite decreases and you may find she becomes less interested in food generally. Some toddlers seem to survive on virtually nothing, even though they are constantly on the move. This is a normal response to the slowdown in growth that occurs in the second year of life. Between birth and 12 months, the average weight gain is 6kg, but between 12 and 24 months it is just 2.5kg. Because your baby's weight isn't increasing as fast, her food intake doesn't need to keep on rising, as it did from six to 12 months. Although a slump in appetite is normal, make sure that your toddler isn't filling up on milk or juice between meals, instead of eating her food.

> 66 Liam ate very well as a baby, but at about 18 months he became really fussy. First he refused my homemade meals and would only eat jars. Then he went off jars too. I tried giving him the same as the other kids, but he was having none of it. He's dreadful now – he won't eat any vegetables,

although he eats fruit. He eats bread mainly and he'll have bananas and yogurt, but he picks at anything else. **99**
Lisa, mum to Ciara, 10 years, Sean, 6 years and Liam, 2 years

Dealing with power struggles

As your one-year-old becomes increasingly independent and vocal, she's likely to let you know quite clearly what she does and doesn't want to eat and when she's had enough. Now is the time when food battles are more likely to occur, especially if you try to get your toddler to eat more than she wants to. In other areas of life you have the ultimate control: you can pick her up so that she can't climb up the stairs or take away a pen if she's chewing on it. But when it comes to eating, she is in control. As soon as babies learn the word 'no', it can become a firm favourite and power struggles start to become quite common for some one-year-olds.

TIP You can't *make* your baby eat – and you shouldn't try to. Babies often seem to eat less at this stage as their growth slows down. There is very little you can do, and any attempt is likely to be counter-productive.

The best thing you can do is to continue offering a variety of healthy foods and keep meal times as relaxed and pleasant as possible. It's up to your toddler whether she eats her food or leaves it.

A good way to avert bad behaviour at meal times is to distract a toddler. If food is being spat out just for fun, you could point out something interesting outside the window or chat about the noises that different animals make. If meals aren't eaten, then clear up with a minimum of fuss.

Try to resist offering alternatives, as this can be a slippery slope that leads to you cooking a different meal for each member of the family. Games, such as pretending spoonfuls of dinner are aeroplanes coming in to land, can also escalate, so that in the end there's more playing than eating. Likewise, suggesting a toddler eats one spoonful for daddy, then one for granny, and so on, isn't a good idea. Coaxing, nagging and bribery are common tactics used by parents to encourage children to eat. But none of them is really effective; children should be eating because they're hungry, and once meal-time patterns like this begin, they can be difficult to change. Try to remember that healthy children don't starve themselves.

Encourage your baby to feed herself

Toddlers don't need to be fed by a parent at every meal. When your one-year-old has food, such as porridge, that needs to be eaten with a spoon, give her one. She might need help loading it or you might want to have another spoon yourself too, but she should be encouraged to feed herself as much as possible. Don't worry about the mess until the end of a meal. And as soon as she can manage on her own then let her.

Some meals, such as sandwiches and salad, are best eaten with hands; others, such as roast dinner, will probably be eaten with a spoon and fork as well as with hands. You can give your baby a little knife if you want to but most toddlers won't really be able to use it yet. Self-feeding skills will become more refined but it takes a while.

It's fine if your toddler wants to eat with her hands rather than use cutlery. You don't want to put her off her food by forcing her to use a spoon.

By about 18 months, self-feeding with a spoon is usually fairly efficient, although the spoon is still held in the fist like a stick, rather than between the fingers like a pen, which is what most adults do.

As toddlers become more mobile and start to move around and walk, the idea of sitting in a highchair can seem less appealing. Some may be pleased to be put in their highchair to eat, but others struggle to get away before their food even appears. They seem to see meal times as an inconvenient interruption in their busy schedule.

TIP If your toddler isn't keen on meal times, try to make the transition from playing to highchair as easy as possible. Make a game of chasing your toddler into the kitchen or sing a song as you wash hands. Then it doesn't seem like the fun is suddenly stopping because it's time to eat.

As with most things, there's a balance to be struck. Meal times aren't just about eating as quickly as possible. They should also be an enjoyable time to be together and chat. However, too much fun can be distracting, especially for those who are slow eaters. You have to see what works best for your child.

The most effective tactics to encourage healthy eating are to share meals, so that she can see you enjoying your food, and to continue to offer healthy foods, whether or not they're eaten. Your toddler will now take a lot more notice of what you are doing and will want to imitate you, so if you want her to eat her peas, let her see you eating yours. Of course, not all toddlers are fussy eaters. If yours is continuing to eat well, then make the most of this spirit of adventure. Offer as much variety as possible, then if fussiness creeps in later she'll still have a reasonably good diet.

A balanced diet for a toddler

Now that your baby has passed her first birthday, you can offer her an even wider range of foods.

Each day try to offer your toddler:

- three or four servings of starchy foods (e.g. breakfast cereal, bread, pasta and potatoes)
- four or five servings of fruit and vegetables
- two servings of meat, fish, eggs or pulses
- 300–350ml milk or about two servings of yogurt or cheese. Cows' milk can now be introduced as your baby's main drink if she is eating well.

As you can see, a healthy diet for your baby is starting to look more like a healthy adult diet. Your baby needs a lot less milk than before and she should be eating more fruit and vegetables. Just as adults need their 'five a day' when it comes to fruit and vegetables, the same applies to toddlers. Yours may have developed some favourites by now, such as carrots and bananas, but continue trying to give a wide range of different-coloured varieties every day.

While your toddler's meals can start to resemble yours more closely, she still needs less fibre, so it's best not to give too many foods such as very high-fibre breakfast cereals. Your toddler also needs more fat in her diet than you, so she should still have full-fat versions of dairy products, such as milk, yogurt and cheese. Between the ages of two and five, children can gradually move to the kind of low-fat, high-fibre diet we think of as healthy for adults.

Junk food and IQ

You may have read headlines saying that eating junk food lowers a toddler's IQ. These worrying articles were generated by research carried out at the University of Bristol. Scientists studying large numbers of children found that diets high in fat, sugar and processed foods at age three were linked with lower IQ scores at age eight. Diets packed full of vitamins and minerals appeared to have the opposite effect.

They divided the children into different groups according to the type of foods they typically ate and found that those with a 'health conscious' pattern – who ate salad, fruit, vegetables, rice and pasta – seemed to fare best. Interestingly, they found that what the children ate when they were four or seven years old didn't have the same impact on IQ. It appeared that even if children's diets improved after the age of three, the negative effects of a 'junk food' pattern of eating seemed to persist. The researchers suggested that this might be because the brain grows at its fastest rate in the first three years of life, and that good nutrition during this period may encourage optimal growth. So if a child eats badly at this time, it can have long-term effects.

Keep an eye on the iron

Most toddlers don't get enough iron. About 6% of children between 18 and 30 months old are clinically anaemic, and many more will be mildly anaemic. To ensure your toddler gets all the iron she needs, the first thing to do is check she isn't having too much milk. This can prevent her from having a good intake of meat, fish and vegetables. Also, stick with an iron-fortified breakfast cereal most days. Some toddlers are just more prone to anaemia, but, in general, those who consume more iron have higher levels of it in their blood. It's very difficult to tell if a toddler is anaemic, as in mild cases some children don't show any symptoms.

Others can appear pale and generally lacking in energy. They may become breathless when they run around and be more prone to illness and infections. The only way to be sure if a toddler is anaemic is with a blood test, so if you are concerned you should talk to your doctor or health visitor.

Salt's still an issue

Now, you don't have to be quite so careful about salt. Before 12 months, babies could have no more than 1g of salt per day, but between one and three years the upper limit is raised to 2g of salt per day. Despite the limit being doubled, you do still need to be vigilant, as most toddlers have more salt than recommended and children as young as four have been found to have raised blood pressure because of their high salt intakes. It is best to avoid high-salt foods such as sausages and other processed meat products. You should also avoid children's foods, such as potato shapes and cheese spreads, as they tend to have a high salt content.

If you buy commercially prepared foods for your toddler, you need to look carefully at the label to check the salt content. Whereas meals for babies under a year don't usually have salt added, those suitable from 12 months sometimes can have quite a high salt content. There is a big difference between different brands, so careful checking really is the only answer.

> TIP Keep the saltcellar off the table, and don't use it on your food in view of your toddler if you can help it. Otherwise your toddler will be tempted to copy you and try it out.

Other foods to avoid

As well as being careful about your toddler's salt intake, you should continue to watch out for choking hazards. Whole nuts shouldn't be given until the age of five. You should also avoid giving swordfish, marlin and shark, as they can contain high levels of mercury, which could damage the nervous system as your child continues to grow.

> TIP As your toddler's intestines are now more developed, it is fine to give her honey.

Meals for your toddler

Now is the time when eating patterns become more firmly established. So toddlers should be in the habit of having three meals every day, with a maximum of two healthy snacks.

We know that many children fall into poor eating habits in the pre-school years, with constant snacking or grazing, and eating meals made up of high-fat and high-sugar foods, particularly processed ones. In fact, as many as 23% of children start school either overweight or obese, which highlights how serious this issue is. Encouraging healthy dietary patterns and giving plenty of opportunities for physical activity are both important for keeping your toddler at a healthy weight. But you also have to be wary of being unnecessarily strict.

> TIP There is no need to deny your toddler a chocolate biscuit if everyone else is having one at playgroup or not allow her to go to a tea party. Having foods like this occasionally is fine.

Research shows that restricting children's access to specific foods, along with pressuring children to eat, is counter-productive, and can lead to children developing an unhealthy relationship with food. It seems that banning certain foods can lead to those foods becoming more desirable, so a balanced approach is needed. Foods such as cakes, chocolate and crisps should be seen as something to have only occasionally. If you know you eat these kinds of foods too often, now is a good time to cut down, otherwise the chances are your toddler will follow suit.

Breakfast

Breakfast is an important meal for your toddler, and fortified breakfast cereals can make a significant contribution to her vitamin and iron intake. You might want to look back at the breakfast ideas in Chapter

7 (see p134) as these are just as good now. As your toddler gets older she might be drawn to the child-friendly packaging of sugar-coated or chocolate-flavoured cereals, but try to stick to plainer cereals.

> TIP Make plain cereals more interesting by adding foods such as dried apricots or raisins, sliced strawberries or banana, or a dollop of yogurt.

If you find your toddler goes off breakfast, then make sure she hasn't filled up on too much milk. Maybe try leaving a gap between her drink and breakfast. Tea and coffee are not suitable for toddlers and having these with breakfast can interfere with iron absorption. If your toddler really doesn't want to eat breakfast, make sure you have some healthy foods ready for later on, so that she doesn't just have a muffin in the shops or biscuits at playgroup instead. If she eats lots of unhealthy snacks it will have a knock-on effect, reducing her appetite for lunch.

Ideas for breakfast on the go

- Peanut butter and banana sandwich
- Oatcakes with cream cheese
- Hot cross bun with cream cheese
- Dry cereal (e.g. Shreddies or Cheerios) plus a banana
- Cream cheese sandwich (with dried apricot or raisins)
- Apple and carrot muffin (see p177) plus a satsuma

Lunch and dinner

When you're thinking about what to give your toddler for lunch or dinner, try to work out what dishes you can eat together. This should now be a lot easier. At this age, she can eat a wide range of foods and she'll be getting better all the time at feeding herself. All the meal ideas in this chapter of the book are for the whole family to enjoy.

It is much better for your toddler to move on to healthy, unprocessed adult meals than to start eating 'children's foods'. Meals that are typically marketed for children tend to contain the poorest-quality ingredients, including the cheapest cuts of meat and the least amount of vegetables. Beige seems to be the predominant colour for children's food, and while your child may be given foods like chicken nuggets and potato waffles by friends at some point, try to stick to colourful unprocessed foods as far as possible. Moving from baby food to 'kids' food' is all too often a backwards step in nutritional terms and there is no reason why this has to be the case.

> 66 *Alfie absolutely loves any kind of fish and has done since he first had it as a baby. When I'm in a hurry it's very easy to just pop a piece of haddock or salmon in the microwave for him. It's very quick and I know I'm giving him something healthy.* 99
> **Sara, mum to Alfie, 14 months**

As your toddler gets older there is no reason why she can't continue to eat cooked meals for lunch every day, or at least on some days. Parents who eat later than their baby in the evening may find that keeping some of last night's dinner for their toddler's lunch works well. You might also find that your toddler gradually wants to eat more like you, or other children, which often means eating sandwiches. This can make lunches simpler to prepare and it can also mean that eating in the park or with friends becomes easier.

Sandwiches can be very healthy, but it's easy to end up having the same filling every day, so try to have plenty of variety. The box below has some suggestions for different fillings. You can boost your toddler's vegetable intake by adding some sliced tomato or cucumber to sandwiches. Or you can put some salad or vegetable sticks beside the sandwich. It's also good to buy different types of bread, including wholemeal bread, granary bread, rolls, panini, pitta and wraps. Toasted sandwiches also make a nice change.

Tasty sandwich fillings

- Tuna with mayonnaise and cucumber or sweetcorn
- Cheese and coleslaw
- Houmous and avocado or grated carrot
- Peanut butter, grated carrot and cucumber
- Cream cheese and avocado
- Grated cheese and cucumber
- Cheddar cheese and tomato
- Sliced hard-boiled egg with tomato
- Chicken and salad
- Egg mayonnaise and cress
- Roast beef and tomato
- Sardine pâté (mashed sardine, cream cheese and tomato purée) with cucumber
- Mashed sardine with chopped egg
- Tinned salmon and cucumber

Toasties and melts

- Pizza toast (tomato purée and cheddar)
- Tuna melt (tuna and cheddar)
- Mushroom melt (tomato purée or passata, lightly fried mushrooms and cheddar)
- Cheese and sliced tomato toastie
- Mashed sardines (tinned in tomato sauce)
- Mashed sardines (tinned in oil) with lemon juice
- Mackerel pâté (see p157)

If your toddler is keen on sandwiches and toasties, then make the most of it and use them as a way of increasing her intake of other foods, such as oily fish and pulses. If the smell of cooking fish puts you off, then you might find that putting fish, such as tuna and sardines, in sandwiches or on toast works well for you.

TIP If your toddler is reluctant to try new sandwich fillings, make two or three different sandwiches and pack a picnic to take to the park. Eating in the fresh air is more relaxing and fun, and if she feels less pressured to eat she'll be more likely to give them a go.

The recipes in this section are one-pot dishes that are very quick and easy to prepare. They are meals that the whole family can enjoy and they're included here to give you ideas for meals you might not usually make. Meals such as cottage pie (see p156), pasta bolognaise, fish pie and chicken stir-fry are popular family dishes. Remember not to add salt when you're cooking, and if you need stock it's best to make your own or get some low-salt stock cubes. If you find yourself getting into a bit of a rut and cooking the same meals all the time, there are some very good websites that you can look at for inspiration, including netmums.com and bbcgoodfood.com. You don't need to follow recipes exactly, and if you like the sound of a recipe but know it's not terribly healthy, you can probably adapt it. Most recipes still work fine with a health makeover. As well as tweaking new recipes, you can do the same with old favourites.

How to give your favourite recipes a health makeover

- Leave out the salt
- Use low-salt stock cubes
- Cut down on the amount of oil or butter
- Leave out cream or replace it with milk and a bit of cornflour if needed
- Add extra vegetables and take out some of the meat
- Add garlic, herbs or lemon juice for extra flavour

Kids' favourites made healthy

If you have older children who enjoy meals like chicken nuggets or burgers and chips, your toddler will probably want to join in sooner or later. You can make meals like this more healthy for everyone by making them at home. It's not as difficult as you might think.

- **Chicken nuggets** are easy to make by simply dipping pieces of chicken in beaten egg and then breadcrumbs. Then cook them on a baking tray in a preheated oven (200°C/400°F/gas mark 6) for 15 to 20 minutes.
- **Burgers** can be made by mixing minced beef with an egg. Take lumps of the mixture and form burger shapes. Then cook them, just as you would with shop-bought burgers. You can experiment by adding finely chopped onion, tomato purée and herbs, according to your family's taste. When you make your own burgers, you have the advantage of being able to make different-sized burgers for different-sized members of the family. You can also buy whatever type of meat you like – lean minced or organic steak, or even lamb or turkey instead of beef.
- **Burger buns** are traditionally white but there's no reason you shouldn't use granary instead or half a wholemeal pitta bread.
- **Chips** can be made with potatoes that are peeled or left unpeeled and just scrubbed. Slice them into fat chip shapes or wedges and put them in a food bag with a tablespoon of vegetable oil. Shake the bag to coat the chips then put them on a baking tray in a preheated oven (200°C/400°F/gas mark 6) for about 30 minutes. For an even easier option, buy frozen oven chips that contain just potatoes and sunflower oil (check the ingredients label). Some chips and wedges in the shops contain quite a lot of salt, so be careful.
- **Pizza** isn't generally an unhealthy option, unless you choose varieties such as pepperoni. As it has lots of cheese, which is high in salt and saturated fat, it shouldn't be eaten too often. The advantage of making your own is that you can add vegetables. If you're getting shop-bought ones, look for those with the lowest salt content.

By giving meals like this with corn on the cob or salad on the side, you're providing your child with a fairly balanced meal while still giving them what they want.

Chickpea biriyani

1 tablespoon vegetable oil
1 onion (chopped)
2 cloves garlic (crushed)
½ red pepper (diced)
½ green pepper (diced)
2 carrots (diced)
3–4 mushrooms (sliced)
1 heaped tablespoon mild curry powder
1 tin chickpeas (400g)
1 cup basmati rice (approx. 175g)

Preparation time: 30 minutes
Pans: 1
Storage: Suitable for freezing; keeps in the fridge for up to 24 hours.
Serves: Two adults and one or two children.

- Heat the oil in a pan. Add the onion and garlic and sauté for a few minutes then add the other vegetables and cook for five to 10 minutes.
- Mix in the curry powder and continue cooking for a minute.
- Rinse the rice then add it to the pan, along with the chickpeas. Add enough water to cover.
- Put a lid on the pan and bring to the boil, then simmer for 12 to 15 minutes until the rice is ready and the liquid has been absorbed.
- Stir occasionally to make sure it doesn't stick to the bottom of the pan and add extra water if necessary.

Tips

- Serve with chopped cucumber, chopped tomatoes and natural yogurt.
- Instead of chickpeas you can use black-eyed beans, haricot beans or cannellini beans. If possible, buy chickpeas or beans without added salt, otherwise rinse them in cold water.
- You can make this basic recipe with other vegetables, including diced courgette, aubergine or frozen peas.
- If you are keeping some for another day, make sure you cool it and put it in the fridge within an hour, to prevent food poisoning.
- If you want to spice up your meal a bit, you can eat it with spicy mango chutney or raw onion.

Family fish Stew

1 tablespoon vegetable oil
1 onion (diced)
1 leek (diced)
2 cloves garlic (crushed)
2 medium potatoes (peeled and diced)
1 tin chopped tomatoes (400g)
2 tablespoons tomato purée
1 tablespoon mixed herbs
1 bay leaf
½ teaspoon turmeric
1 low-salt stock cube, made up with 500ml water
Black pepper
400g raw fish (e.g. salmon, haddock or coley)
Fresh parsley (finely chopped)
½ lemon

Preparation time: 1 hour
Pans: 1
Storage: Suitable for freezing; keeps in the fridge for up to 24 hours.
Serves: Two adults and one or two children.

- Heat the oil in a large pan. Add the onion, leek and garlic, cover and leave to sweat for three minutes.
- Add the potatoes, tomatoes, tomato purée, herbs, bay leaf, turmeric and stock. Bring to the boil and simmer for 45 minutes until soft.
- Chop the fish into cubes, checking for bones as you cut it.
- Stir the fish into the pan, bring back to the boil and simmer for five minutes until the fish is cooked. Serve with a squeeze of lemon juice and a sprinkle of parsley and black pepper.

Tips

- By using an ordinary stock cube you'll add about 4g of salt to the dish, but a low-salt stock cube instead will add less than 0.2g of salt
- Tinned mackerel can be used in place of some of the fresh fish
- To make a more substantial meal for adults, serve with crusty bread
- If you want to mush a portion with a blender for your baby, make sure you take the bay leaf out first

Puddings and treats

Most babies are happy to eat fresh fruit, fruit purée, yogurt and fromage frais for pudding, but as they become older, sooner or later they'll want something a bit more exciting. Traditional puddings such as rice pudding and fruit crumble can be quite healthy and are very easy to make. Alternatively, you can try the recipes here, which are just more exciting variations along the fruit and yogurt theme. If you do give them cakes or other sugary treats, then keep the portion small and put it on a plate with some fruit. Little tricks like this can ensure your toddler reaches her 'five a day' without a great effort.

Berry delight

250g fresh or frozen raspberries or mixed berries
250g natural yogurt
1 tablespoon dark brown sugar

Preparation time: 5 minutes
Storage: Keeps in the fridge for up to 24 hours.
Serves: Two adults and one or two children.

- Put the berries in a bowl and carefully spoon the yogurt over them.
- Crumble the sugar over the yogurt and leave to dissolve for a few minutes.

Rainbow knickerbocker glory

Kiwi fruit (quartered and sliced)
Strawberries (chopped)
Grapes (halved)
Natural yogurt
Flaked almonds (optional)

Preparation time: 10 minutes
Storage: Best eaten fresh, but keeps in the fridge for up to 24 hours.

- In glass or clear plastic dishes, place alternate layers of fruit and yogurt.
- Sprinkle flaked almonds on the top and add a piece of strawberry or grape for decoration.

Tips

- You can make this with any fruit you like – the more colourful the better
- Fruit purée or tinned peaches, apricots or mango could also be used

Apple and carrot muffins

175g self-raising flour
5ml bicarbonate of soda
100g soft brown sugar
2 eggs
100ml oil (rapeseed or sunflower)
100g grated carrot
100g grated apple
75g chopped dried apricots
25g chopped walnuts (or raisins)

Preparation time: 40 minutes (including 10–15 minutes in the oven)
Pans: 1 mixing bowl plus 2 muffin trays with paper cake cases
Storage: Keep in an airtight container for up to 3 days. Also suitable for freezing.
Servings: Makes 16 muffins, but if you want to make some smaller muffins simply divide the mixture between a larger number of cake cases.

- Pour the oil into a mixing bowl and beat in the eggs. Then mix in the grated apple and carrot and the chopped apricots and nuts.
- Next, stir in the flour, bicarbonate of soda and sugar.
- Spoon the mixture into the cake cases and bake at 180°C/350°F/gas mark 4 for 10–15 minutes.

Tips

- For a special treat, you can put icing on the top, made by mixing 150g icing sugar, 10g margarine and 50g cream cheese

Snacks: make every bite count

Snacks make a significant contribution to a toddler's nutrient intake. If your toddler doesn't eat much at meal times, it can be tempting to offer her biscuits and other treats, thinking that it's better she eats anything rather than nothing. However, it is much better to keep to three regular meal times and two snack times a day. If she doesn't eat meals, try to get on with other activities and resist chasing your toddler around, constantly offering her more food.

When snack time arrives, make sure that the foods you offer are as healthy as possible. This is a time to eat foods containing the nutrients that were missed earlier.

> TIP Make sure your toddler doesn't fill up on unhealthy things like biscuits, which provide calories without supplying the vitamins and minerals she needs.

If toddlers eat between meals, it inevitably leads to them being too full for the next meal. Also, children soon learn that if they don't feel like eating the meal on offer, they can leave it and have biscuits instead. Bad habits are very easily formed but hard to break, so try to avoid an unhealthy snacking pattern developing. Instead, make every bite count.

The best snacks for a toddler day to day are just the same as those for a baby: fresh fruit and starchy foods, such as plain breadsticks. If your toddler isn't eating much at meal times, then snacks that are more like mini meals might be a good idea, for example a cream cheese sandwich and vegetable sticks.

Dried fruits are full of vitamins and minerals, but remember they are sticky and stay on the teeth for a long time, so eating them frequently isn't good for dental health. It may be better to give your toddler foods such as raisins and apricots after a meal and only occasionally as a snack.

Healthy snacking

Everyday snacks

- A banana
- Mini cream cheese sandwich
- Mini houmous sandwich
- Breadsticks
- Rice cakes (no added salt)
- Pot of fresh fruit (kiwi, halved grapes or satsuma)
- Dry breakfast cereal
- Cheese
- Raw vegetable sticks (cucumber or carrot)

Occasional snacks

- Raisins
- Dried apricots
- Dried figs
- Malt loaf
- Plain biscuits

Drinks

Once babies reach 12 months old, most can start to have cows' milk as their main drink and cut down from having 500–600ml a day to just 300–350ml. However, some babies aren't ready yet. If your baby isn't eating many iron-rich foods, you may wish to continue with formula for a few more months, rather than switching to cows' milk, which has a lower iron content. Formula is available specifically for toddlers from 12 months but it hasn't been shown to be beneficial – and it costs about three times as much as fresh cows' milk. You can give this type of formula if you would like to, but, as with follow-on milks for babies over six months, there is no need (see p124).

Once you make the switch to cows' milk it should be the full-fat version for at least the next year. Semi-skimmed milk is only suitable for toddlers over two years of age, and then only if they are having a good diet. Skimmed milk isn't suitable as a main drink until children are five years old.

> TIP When toddlers move from formula to cows' milk their intake of vitamin D drops dramatically, so if your toddler hasn't been taking vitamin drops she should start to take them now (see p17).

How much do toddlers need?

As toddlers have less milk than before, it's important to make sure they still get plenty of fluids. It is estimated that toddlers need at least a litre of fluids a day or about 100ml of fluids per kilogram of body weight. This works out at about eight 120ml drinks a day. If your toddler has milk in the morning and at bedtime, she still needs a drink with each meal and at least one more between each meal time. You might think water is a bit boring as your toddler gets older, and be tempted to offer juice or squash, but water is still the best drink for her.

Toddlers can easily become dehydrated, which can result in them becoming confused, irritable and lethargic. These signs might be difficult to spot, but if your toddler is especially cranky, bear in mind that dehydration could be a factor. As your toddler may be too busy to think about drinking between meals, make sure she has a cup of water when she stops for a meal or snack. It's particularly important to give cups of water regularly in hot weather or when your toddler has been very active. Another problem can be distinguishing hunger cues from those for thirst. Sometimes you might think your toddler is hungry when she is actually thirsty, so it might be better to offer water first.

> 66 He wouldn't have had juice if it wasn't for our darn nanny. She looks after another kid who has juice, so it was hard for her to do as I'd asked, and not give it to him. He only gets water at home but he asks for apple juice all the time! 99
> **Kent, dad to Paul, 23 months**

Bottle dependence

It is best to give all drinks in a cup now rather than a bottle. This is especially important for fruit drinks (see p21), but from 12 months babies should also be having their milk in a cup. If you have been breastfeeding up to now, but are planning to stop, then there is no need to give a bottle at all. Your baby can move directly to having milk from a cup.

If your toddler is very attached to her bottle of milk and doesn't want to move to a cup, it can be difficult to know what to do. Some parents make their toddler go cold turkey, and just take the bottle away completely. But if this isn't for you, you can try to make the transition easier by keeping the bottle for bedtime, when your toddler is likely to want the comfort, but give her a cup during the day.

> TIP If your toddler has a bottle at bedtime she should drink it before you put her down rather than having it to fall asleep with.

Some toddlers decide by themselves when they don't want a bottle anymore, but it can get harder to break the bottle habit as they get older, so it's worth persevering now. Another problem can be that toddlers who use their bottle of milk for comfort, particularly at bedtime, can end up getting more calories than they need. Research has shown that toddlers who still drink from a bottle at 24 months are 30% more likely to be obese when they start school.

Squash drinking syndrome

Drinking lots of high-energy drinks, such as fruit juice and squash, can result in toddlers suffering from a poor appetite, irritability, diarrhoea and inadequate weight gain. The term 'squash drinking syndrome' was first coined in the 1990s when an increasing amount of soft drinks started being consumed by young children. Some pre-schoolers were found to be getting more than 30% of their calories from fruit drinks and it was recognised that these children suffered from a common set of symptoms. Some had undergone a whole host of medical tests, as their parents and doctors were inevitably concerned about their health. Once the link was made with their drinking habits, parents were able to tackle the problem effectively. They reduced their toddlers' intake of fruit drinks and found their symptoms improved and their weight started increasing.

Toddler meal plan

In addition to the meals and snacks in the plan, toddlers should have a cup of milk when they wake up. Toddlers don't need milk in the afternoon, but many still have some at bedtime. They need only 300–350ml of milk a day and can usually get this from a morning bottle plus milk on cereal and foods such as cheese and yogurt.

Your baby will also need a cup of water with each meal and snack. She should also be having vitamin drops (see p17).

Day	Breakfast	Snack	Lunch	Snack	Dinner
1	Shreddies with milk Dried apricot	Breadsticks Grapes cut in half	Mashed sardines on toast and carrot and cucumber sticks Fruit flapjack	Mini peanut butter sandwich	Chickpea biriyani with yogurt (see p174) Fruit salad
2	Porridge made with milk Half a banana	Satsuma	Wrap with avocado, houmous, cucumber and tomato Fromage frais	Apple and carrot muffin (see p177)	Shepherd's pie and broccoli Rhubarb crumble and custard
3	Hot oat cereal with milk Half a slice of toast with peanut butter	Small pear	Lemony lentil dip (see p155) with pitta bread, tomato and apple	Rice cake and a fruit pouch	Stir-fried strips of pork, mushroom, red pepper and baby corn with noodles Banana, yogurt and flaked almonds

4	Peanut butter and banana sandwich	Cheesy scone fingers (see p141)	Mackerel pâté (see p157) on toast and cucumber sticks Peach	Fig roll biscuit	Pasta with bolognaise made from Quorn mince and vegetables, plus grated cheese Berry delight (see p176)
5	Weetabix with milk Sliced mango	Scone fingers (see p141) and apple wedges	Pasta with avocado, cottage cheese and peas	Vegetable sticks and houmous	Chicken leg and couscous with frozen mixed vegetables Oaty pancake, fruit compote or purée and dairy ice cream
6	French toast fingers and mashed banana and yogurt	Oat cakes with cream cheese	Couscous salad with chicken, peppers and cucumber	Small peach	Family fish stew (see p175) French bread Apple and carrot muffin
7	Oaty pancakes (see p152), scrambled eggs and halved cherry tomatoes	Two plums	Houmous and grated carrot sandwich and roast vegetable sticks Strawberries and yogurt	Cream cheese sandwiches	Homemade burger (see p173), oven chips (see p173) and salad Rice pudding with pear

This meal plan has been designed to ensure it meets a one to two-year-old toddler's requirements for energy, protein, potassium, calcium, magnesium, phosphorus, iron, copper, zinc, chloride, selenium, iodine, thiamin, riboflavin, niacin, folic acid and vitamins A, B6, B12, C and E. Also, each day's menu contains less than 2g of salt, which is the maximum amount a toddler this age should have each day.

Like the previous menu plan (see p159), it isn't meant to be followed exactly but will hopefully give you some ideas about the types of foods that will make up a healthy diet for your toddler.

Part three
Special diets and common problems

In Part three you'll find lots of practical advice about tackling the all-too-common problem of fussy eating. There's also information about what to do if you think your baby might have an allergy or any other kind of bad reaction to food. Then we look at some other fairly common problems: reflux (when food or acid comes back up), constipation and anaemia. There's also specific advice for premature babies and nutrition guidance for vegetarian babies.

10

Combatting fussy eating

If you're worried that your baby isn't eating enough or that she's not having the foods that are good for her, the first thing to do is to look at it objectively. Feeding your baby can be an emotional matter, but try to take a step back while you consider two issues.

Firstly, look at your baby's growth and general health. If your health visitor or GP is happy with her growth and she seems to be well and happy, then there is less of a problem.

The second issue is what your baby is eating. You might be thinking that is easy to answer, because she doesn't eat anything. However, it is quite normal for a baby's appetite to vary considerably from day to day. To get a clearer picture of what your baby really is eating, write down everything she has for three days – including the crust of dad's sandwich, the biscuit granny gave her and the extra milk you thought she needed to make sure she'd sleep. All the little bits can add up, and when you see things written down you might find that actually she's not eating too badly. Or, you might see a picture emerging that shows she's eating, but not the foods you want her to eat. You might also be able to identify problem areas, such as too much milk or too many rusks.

66 *Julia started solids at five and a half months old and enjoyed her food, but between seven and nine months she hardly ate anything. She was very fussy. It was really stressful and I remember crying and I was losing hair. She might eat just one spoonful then stop. I gave her extra milk but the health visitor said not to, so I stopped and very gradually from about 10 months she started eating more. She's not a big eater now but she's fine.* 99
Arleta, mum to Julia, 15 months

My baby won't eat anything

If your baby won't eat, it can be both frustrating and upsetting. It is also very easy to blame yourself for your baby's poor eating habits. However, it's important to remember that all babies are different and some are just pickier about their food than others. It's helpful to think about what fussy eating really is. There are certain foods all of us avoid, but we don't see it as a big problem. It is only when a whole range of foods isn't eaten that it can become a concern.

The most common reasons for a poor appetite are:

- too much milk (babies need no more than 600ml a day and toddlers no more than 350ml)
- too many snacks between meals
- too many fruit drinks
- distractions at meal times, such as TV or other people who aren't eating
- too much pressure to eat
- not enough time and feeling rushed
- lots of attention for not eating.

Most of these are fairly obvious, but because you're worrying about your baby's health and whether you are failing in your role as a good parent, it can be hard to see what's really going on. The first thing to think about is what your baby is having between meals, which may be filling her up and leaving her too full at meal times. As babies have small tummies, this can happen easily and can lead to a vicious circle. You worry your baby hasn't eaten her breakfast, so you give her a couple of biscuits but then she's too full for her lunch, so she either doesn't eat much or just eats her favourite bits.

When a baby goes off her food the best thing to do is not to get stressed, however hard that may seem. If you can't manage it, at least try to appear relaxed to your baby. If you start trying to force-feed her or make a big fuss, it could actually create a problem where there really was none. A baby may not eat much for a few days because she has sore gums or feels under the weather. She's then likely to go back to her usual eating habits. However, if she was fussed over and got a lot of attention for not eating, she might be less likely to start eating again and instead see meal times as a horrible experience or a time to watch mummy jump around and play aeroplanes.

> ❝ I remember Max opening his mouth wide right from the start, but Zoe was a different story altogether. I tried to wean her at six months but she would have none of it, and her weight was going down percentiles. I realise now, two years later, how foolish I was to worry – if you're human you will get hungry and, eventually, you will eat. It's hard to take that in when you're in the thick of it of course. ❞
> **Jasmin, mum to Max, 4 years and Zoe, 2 years**

If your baby doesn't eat something, or even if she eats absolutely nothing, stay calm and avoid exacerbating the situation. You may well be worried and tempted to offer a string of alternatives in desperation, but do try to hold back. Some people withhold pudding if a meal isn't eaten or don't give any snacks between meals, but this isn't necessarily a good idea. If pudding is something nutritious, such as fruit and yogurt, there seems no benefit in keeping it from your baby. That said, don't give an enormous portion to compensate for the uneaten dinner, and do make sure the pudding is nutritious. Your baby shouldn't be having a big bowl of chocolate pudding instead of fish and vegetables.

Likewise, still offer snacks between meals, but make sure they provide the nutrients your baby missed out on earlier. You can do this perhaps by giving her foods such as mini houmous sandwiches and vegetable sticks. It can be tempting to give a biscuit to a baby who hasn't eaten lunch, thinking she needs it, but if she has a poor appetite there is even more reason not to. Snacks like this will just fill her up without providing the nutrients she needs. It's better to give a small healthy snack (see p179) and, if necessary, give her an evening meal a little earlier. If there are particular foods that tend to be left uneaten, such as vegetables, you can try offering these as finger foods at the beginning of the meal when she's hungrier.

Here are some ways to encourage good eating habits.

- Eat with your baby so she can see you enjoying your food.
- Don't worry if your baby doesn't eat much some days and don't offer alternatives.
- Keep offering a range of healthy foods whether or not they are eaten.
- Praise your baby for eating well but ignore what isn't eaten.
- Offer only small healthy snacks between meals – make every bite count.
- Make sure your baby isn't having too much milk or juice.

It's very easy to fall into bad habits. If you're reading this and thinking 'I do that', don't worry. These are very natural reactions. We all want the best for our babies, and giving them food, any food that they'll eat, seems like the right thing. However, the short-term satisfaction of seeing your baby eating something, or having an extra bottle of milk, needs to be weighed up against the long-term goal of helping her develop good eating habits. It's easier to do that now before she develops good 'pester power' skills. It is generally the worry that makes parents turn to well-intentioned but unhelpful strategies to encourage their child to eat. So, whatever else you do, remember that your job is not to make your child eat; it's to provide healthy food and a relaxed environment.

> 66 *Edie was OK with purées at the beginning, but then I gave her finger foods and she just went off eating completely. Other babies seemed to be chowing down on whatever they were given, but she refused everything. Getting her to eat is still really difficult and I've found some people can be very judgemental, which makes it worse. I didn't do anything different with my son but he's been much easier – a lot of it's down to luck.* 99
> **Heni, mum to Edie, 4 years and Sholto, 17 months**

My baby's fussy about certain foods

If there are certain major food groups that your baby won't eat, there's a risk that she will miss out on particular nutrients. However, babies often go through phases with their eating habits – loving cheese or bananas for weeks, then going off them completely for a while. This is just something to keep you on your toes, in case you were thinking you'd now got to grips with this parenting thing. However, if your baby does go off particular foods, there are plenty of tactics you can try to help her get as balanced a diet as possible. The tips below should help.

Ten tips for babies who won't drink milk

1. Give your baby some breakfast cereal with milk every morning. One wheat biscuit, like Weetabix, will soak up about 100ml of milk if you leave it for a few minutes.
2. Cook dishes that have milk in them, such as mashed potato, macaroni cheese and fish in white sauce.
3. Remember that cows' milk isn't a suitable drink for babies under 12 months, as it has too much sodium and not enough iron. So if your baby is getting her milk from food, use formula instead of cows' milk. This is easy for cereal, but you can use it in cooking too.
4. Give your baby full-fat dairy products every day, including full-fat yogurt and fromage frais at breakfast time or as a pudding, and cream cheese sandwiches or cubes of cheese as a snack.
5. If you're moving from breastfeeding to bottle-feeding and your baby doesn't want to take formula in a bottle, try giving it in a cup instead.
6. Keep on offering milk as a drink, especially if your baby is under 12 months. If you do this, and don't get stressed if it's not drunk, she may decide to go for it.
7. Try different brands of formula or giving cold milk if your baby doesn't like it warm.
8. To make sure your baby has plenty of fluids, offer water and give foods that naturally contain water, such as fruit.
9. Add cheese to meals such as pasta or give cheese on toast. However, remember cheese is salty (0.2g salt per 2mm thick slice) so don't give too much.

10. Give your baby non-dairy foods that contain calcium, such as mashed sardines, tofu and curly kale.

Ten tips for babies who won't eat vegetables

1. Give vegetables at the start of a meal when your baby is hungrier and might be more likely to have a few mouthfuls.
2. Give vegetables as finger food, then your baby will be able to feel them with her hands and lick them or suck them to become more familiar with them. Some babies are more cautious and this is sometimes a necessary step before they actually eat them.
3. Try different types of vegetables. She might not like broccoli and carrots, but what about parsnips, butternut squash or baby corn?
4. Cook vegetables in different ways. If your baby doesn't seem to like boiled vegetables then try roasting them, which gives a sweeter flavour, or stir fry them. Also, think about whether they are too hard or soft – some babies may find lightly steamed vegetables too hard to eat easily and too much like hard work. Others may prefer their vegetables more crunchy.
5. Add puréed or grated vegetables to foods your baby likes, such as pasta or mashed potato.
6. If vegetables aren't eaten, don't give up. Keep putting them in the bowl or on the highchair tray whenever you cook them for yourself. Vegetables should be a normal part of every lunch and dinner.
7. Give cold vegetables as a snack, for example steamed carrot sticks and baby corn. You may not fancy them yourself but your baby might.
8. Give vegetable sticks with a dip, such as houmous or the lemony lentil dip (p155) or mackerel pâté (p157).
9. Make sure your baby sees you eating and enjoying vegetables.
10. Try doing a joyful 'Cheers!' with your broccoli spear against your baby's, before eating yours up with a smile.

Ten tips for babies who won't eat fruit

1. Instead of buying fruit yogurt, mix your own. A pot of fruit yogurt typically contains just 5% fruit, which in an 85g baby-sized pot is less than a teaspoonful. If you make your own, with half fruit purée and half yogurt, your baby will get 10 times as much fruit.

2. Use fruit purée as a dip. Your baby can dip breadsticks, scone fingers or bits of toast in it.
3. If your baby doesn't like fruit purée, give pieces of fruit as finger food instead. If this doesn't go well you could try giving some yogurt, custard or rice pudding for dipping it in.
4. Try lots of different types of fresh fruit. Some babies don't like citrus fruit, such as oranges, but they like other high vitamin C fruits like kiwi or strawberries. Others don't like hard fruit such as apples, but love peach and melon.
5. Remember that tinned fruit and frozen fruit can be just as good as fresh or puréed.
6. Give fruit as a snack, either chopped up in a pot or whole.
7. Babies and toddlers who don't like fresh fruit sometimes like raisins or other dried fruit, such as apricots or prunes. These can be eaten as they are or added to scones or porridge.
8. Add a bit of fruit to savoury dishes, for example you could chop some dried apricots and add them to chicken casserole.
9. If your baby likes breakfast cereal or porridge, try mixing a bit of fruit with it, such as mashed banana or apple purée.
10. Very cold fruit is sometimes popular with babies who are teething as it can help relieve sore gums. You can freeze half a peeled banana in a freezer bag or put fruit purée in an ice lolly mould to make fruit lollies.

Ten tips for babies who won't eat meat

1. If your baby doesn't like pieces of meat and seems to find them hard to chew, then give meat dishes made with minced meat, such as cottage pie or spaghetti bolognaise. You can also get minced turkey and use that to make a casserole or pasta sauce.
2. Babies who don't like bits of meat in a mixed dish will sometimes eat it as finger food. A chicken leg can be good as it's easy to hold and your baby can suck and chew or gum the meat more slowly.
3. Try different types of meat – red meat has a stronger flavour than chicken and a different texture.
4. Give your baby fish. All fish provides protein and iron, just like meat, and it has the added advantage of containing less saturated fat. By choosing oily fish you'll also be giving your baby long-chain omega 3 fatty acids (see p18).

5. Use meat substitutes such as Quorn mince or soya mince to make dishes such as bolognaise, or pieces of tofu instead of chicken when you're cooking a stir fry.
6. Give alternatives to meat such as chickpeas, beans and lentils more often. These provide many of the same nutrients as meat.
7. Make some new meat dishes. If you usually give particular dishes such as beef in a bolognaise sauce or chicken in a casserole, perhaps it's the overall flavour of the dish that your baby doesn't like, rather than the particular meat itself.
8. Make a meat pâté by puréeing leftover meat dishes such as mince and putting it on toast.
9. Remember that a vegetarian diet can be just as healthy as one containing meat, so don't worry.
10. Look at Chapter 14 on weaning a vegetarian baby to see what nutrients babies can miss out on if they don't eat meat (see p237).

Ten tips for babies who won't drink water

1. Put the water in a cup rather than a bottle. If your baby is used to having warm milk in a bottle, it might be an unpleasant surprise to be given a bottle and finding cold water instead.
2. Try different types of baby cups. It can be hard to get water out of cups with a no-spill spout, so a free-flow one may work better. Also, some cups give water a slightly plastic taste. It's a good idea to give them a go yourself.
3. Give water on a spoon or from an open cup to get your baby used to the flavour or lack of it.
4. Let your baby have plenty of opportunities to play with the cup of water so that she has a chance to get used to it and see how it works.
5. Give fluids in food by making foods as runny as possible, for example by adding cooking water when you make purées.
6. Give foods that naturally contain a high proportion of water. Fruits and vegetables all contain water, but some, for example pears, melon, cucumber and tomatoes, contain more than others.
7. Offer your baby water between meals when she's not so hungry and keen for food.
8. Offer water with every meal and snack, whether or not your baby drinks it. Put the cup to her mouth but also leave it on the table or highchair tray so she can have a go on her own.

9. If your baby or toddler likes milk and is getting all the milk she needs, then add a bit of extra water to her bottle of milk.
10. Keep trying. Babies rarely drink much to start with and that's fine; they'll gradually take more. Don't be tempted to give up and offer fruit juice instead, or it will be very hard to switch to plain water later.

11

Food allergies and intolerances

The number of children suffering from allergies has increased considerably in recent years. It is now estimated that between 6% and 8% of babies in the UK have a food allergy. However, this is only the proportion that has been diagnosed by a healthcare professional. The true number may be much higher. If you're worried your baby has a food allergy you're not alone. More than a third of parents share this suspicion about their child.

The first thing you should do is see your GP or health visitor. Also get as much information about allergies as possible. The internet is the main source for many parents, but whenever you find information about allergies make sure you look at who is running the website. Many advertise completely unreliable but very expensive allergy testing services. So be careful to choose sites offering advice from reliable sources such as the NHS or DoH. Unfortunately, some parents find their concerns about allergies are dismissed by health professionals, but the more information you have, the better chance you have of getting the help your baby needs.

TIP Don't panic. The media usually report only the most severe and life-threatening allergies. However, the majority of allergic reactions are mild.

The big mystery for scientists is why the number of allergies is increasing. There are a number of theories, including the low intake of fruit and vegetables among many children, low levels of vitamin D and increasing intakes of vegetable fats. Another theory is the 'hygiene hypothesis', which suggests babies aren't exposed to enough germs and this affects the normal development of their immune system.

> 66 *I found that when my son went to nursery, they would only give him foods they considered 'allergenic' (wheat, milk, fish, nuts, sesame, eggs) if he had eaten them at home already and had not had a reaction. It's something other parents might not be aware of but find useful to know in preparation for going to nursery.* 99
> **Elizabeth, mum to Kit, 9 months**

What causes allergies?

A food allergy occurs when the body overreacts and mistakenly fights off something that isn't usually considered dangerous. In the case of food allergies, the immune system reacts against something that is eaten. As well as attacking the substance that it thinks is harmful (the allergen), the body also releases other chemicals, particularly histamine, and this causes symptoms such as a rash.

Although nobody understands why this happens, we do know that a baby with a family history of atopy (allergic-type conditions) is at far greater risk. This means a baby is more likely to have an allergy if her mum, dad or any brothers or sisters have an allergy or a condition such as asthma, eczema or hay fever. If your baby has eczema in the first few months of life, it can be an early warning sign that she will have food allergies. It is estimated that 20% of babies with eczema go on to develop a peanut allergy. This may sound somewhat concerning, but remember it means there's an 80% chance they won't.

If a person reacts badly to something they eat, but it isn't caused by the immune system, it is called an intolerance rather than an allergy. For example, cows' milk intolerance results when people don't produce an enzyme that is needed to digest it. It can be hard to distinguish between an allergy and an intolerance when it first occurs, but tests can be used to help diagnose what the problem really is.

The most common causes of food allergies are:

- wheat
- eggs
- milk
- peanuts
- other nuts, e.g. hazelnuts and cashew nuts
- fish
- shellfish
- sesame.

Other foods that sometimes, but less frequently, cause allergies are celery, celeriac, soya, mustard, coconut, pine nuts and kiwi fruit. Although these are the most common causes of allergies, people can be allergic to any food.

How should you introduce new foods?

If your baby has a family history of allergies, there are a few tips that you should bear in mind when you start weaning.

- Introduce the foods that commonly cause allergies only after six months.
- Introduce these foods one at a time so that you can watch for any reaction.
- Avoid introducing these foods in the evening, or at the weekends, when it can be more difficult to get medical help if your baby has a reaction.
- Cook your baby's meals yourself if possible, then you'll know exactly what they contain.
- Make sure that anyone looking after your baby knows which foods she can safely eat and that she shouldn't be given anything else.
- If you are breastfeeding, try to continue while you are weaning, as this appears to reduce the risk of allergies developing as new foods are introduced.

At the moment it is unclear whether babies and young children should avoid foods that could cause allergies. Scientists don't know whether giving high-risk foods early in life actually *increases* or *decreases* the likelihood of an allergy developing. Quite unhelpful!

Avoiding certain foods could mean your baby escapes becoming allergic to them. But, equally, eating them might mean your baby's immune system has the opportunity to learn that these foods are OK. It is thought there is a critical time during a baby's life when the immune system is developing and allergies are more likely to emerge. Large research studies are taking place at the moment to investigate when is the best time to introduce different foods and in what quantities.

The EAT Study (Enquiring About Tolerance), being carried out in London is one project looking at when to introduce certain solids. They are recruiting more than 1,000 babies: half will be weaned at three months and the others at six months. Those weaned early will be given allergenic foods, including peanut butter, eggs, fish, wheat and sesame in increasing quantities at specific times. The other group will follow the current government guidelines on weaning. It will be very interesting to see the results when these two groups of children return to the hospital as one-year-olds and again at three.

This study, along with other research being carried out elsewhere in the UK and in other countries, will help answer the question about whether it is better for babies to avoid or consume certain foods. In the meantime, it is best to follow the current advice regarding weaning.

Does your baby have an allergy?

The most common signs of food allergies are:

- itchy skin or rash
- vomiting
- diarrhoea
- colicky tummy pain
- swollen lips, tongue or mouth
- swollen, red or watery eyes
- sneezing and runny nose
- coughing, wheezing or shortness of breath

- anaphylaxis (a severe reaction involving several of these symptoms and sometimes a loss of consciousness).

Sometimes symptoms can appear within minutes of a baby eating something, but they can take hours or days to develop. If an allergic reaction takes a while to show up, it can be more difficult to identify the exact cause, but you can get round this by keeping a food diary. This involves writing down the different foods that your baby eats each day and recording any symptoms you notice. The important thing to remember is that if a baby has an allergy, she will experience symptoms every time she eats a particular food.

If your baby shows any of the signs listed and you suspect they were caused by something she ate, then you should see your GP or health visitor for advice.

> TIP Don't try to diagnose an allergy yourself or you could end up restricting your baby's diet unnecessarily. If you feel you're not getting all the help you require, then you may need to press for a referral to a consultant.

If signs start to develop straight after your baby has eaten something, try to get medical help immediately. Sometimes symptoms start slowly, for example with lip swelling, but they can then progress to breathing problems, which can be very serious. So, to be on the safe side, it is best to head for a doctor as soon as possible.

Testing for allergies

In 2011, the National Institute for Health and Clinical Excellence (NICE) issued new guidelines about food allergies in children. The guidelines tell GPs and other healthcare professionals how they should go about testing a child when a food allergy is suspected. You can get a copy from the NICE website (www.nice.org.uk).

If you take your baby to see a health professional, the first thing they will do is ask detailed questions about your baby's reactions to food, their general health and their feeding history. If you are breastfeeding then they will ask about your diet too. They should then be able to give you specific advice and decide whether allergy tests are needed. They might say that your baby needs to be referred to an allergy clinic. Generally a combination of different tests is needed to assess whether your child has a food allergy, since no single test can give a conclusive answer. Different tests are useful for investigating different types of reactions, depending on whether they occur immediately or if they are delayed. A severe immediate reaction to a particular food is usually accepted as being pretty conclusive.

The most common allergy tests are described below.

Blood tests

These are sometimes carried out if it is suspected that your baby has an allergy caused by an antibody called immunoglobulin E (IgE). These kinds of allergies usually result in symptoms developing within a few minutes of a person eating a food. Reactions are sudden and might include a rash and swollen lips and eyes or, very rarely, anaphylaxis.

This usually involves taking a blood sample from your baby's arm. The blood is then tested with extracts from different food substances. This makes it possible to test for specific IgE antibodies – which are specific to a particular food. The higher the level found, the more likely it is that a child is allergic to that specific food.

Unfortunately these tests are far from conclusive. Also, even if they show an allergy to a specific food is very likely, they can't tell you how severe an allergic reaction might be. These blood tests are sometimes referred to as RAST (radioallergosorbent) tests.

Skin prick tests

These are also used to help diagnose quick-onset IgE-mediated allergies. If your baby has a skin prick test, a drop of liquid containing the suspect food protein would be put on her arm. The skin would then be pricked – this is a tiny prick and doesn't draw blood. If your baby is allergic to the food, a small red lump will develop within about five to 15 minutes. This disappears quite quickly, usually within about 30 minutes.

> TIP As well as having skin prick tests for foods you suspect your baby has had reactions to, it may be a good idea to test for foods that she hasn't tried yet. That way you'll know what foods to avoid and which ones you can give her, so you won't limit her diet unnecessarily.

Skin patch tests

These are used mainly when a reaction occurs some time after a food is eaten rather than immediately. A solution made from the suspect food is placed on a pad and this is taped to the skin to see if a reaction occurs.

Elimination diets

In an elimination diet, the suspect food or foods are avoided for at least two weeks. During this time any allergy symptoms should disappear. Then your baby is given the suspect food to eat again. If she starts developing the same symptoms again, this suggests that she is indeed allergic to the suspect food.

An elimination diet is usually used when the suspected allergy doesn't result in a sudden reaction but causes symptoms to develop hours or days after the food is eaten. It might show up in long-term problems such as eczema, diarrhoea or constipation. In severe cases, where the allergy hasn't been recognised for some time, it can result in poor growth.

Elimination diets are also useful for diagnosing reactions to food that are not strictly allergic responses, such as an intolerance to high histamine foods or lactose intolerance.

Carrying out an elimination diet for your baby sounds pretty simple, but it needs to be done very carefully. Parents sometimes decide to do it themselves. However, to get an accurate result, you have to be sure that a food is eliminated completely. This means knowing what to look out for on food labels so that your baby doesn't have the suspect food by mistake. For example, if you want to avoid giving your baby egg, you have to make sure you don't give foods containing ingredients such as ovalbumin, which is derived from eggs. You also have to assess your baby's diet as a whole so that she doesn't miss out on certain nutrients as a result of not having a certain food. A specialist should be able to tell you which foods your baby should eat and which to avoid to properly test for an allergy.

Alternative tests

Other tests, including VEGA tests, applied kinesiology and hair analysis are sometimes offered by private clinics and complementary or alternative therapists. These tests are also available on the internet. None of these are considered reliable and the NICE report (2011) recommends that people do not use them. Blood tests known as serum-specific IgG antibody tests are also considered unreliable.

> 66 *Michael had the most revolting nappies, really acidic and offensive. At first we thought he was teething. We tried eliminating dairy and acidic food from his diet but it made no difference. Then we eliminated gluten, which seemed to help a bit. He was losing weight and had blood tests, which were inconclusive. Then after three months his bowel movements returned to normal and two enormous molars appeared. Maybe our initial diagnosis was correct. Anyway, thank goodness he's completely fine now.* 99
> **Kate, mum to Michael, 2 years and Rory, 3 months**

Is there a cure?

At the moment there is no cure for food allergies. However, the good news is that most babies with a food allergy will grow out of it by the time they reach school age. It is estimated that this is the case for as many as 85% of babies with allergies. Those with an allergy to eggs, milk or soya are the most likely to grow out of it. If your baby has an allergy to peanuts or fish, it is more likely to carry on into adulthood.

If your baby is diagnosed with an allergy, regular testing is usually carried out to see if she still has it. This is particularly useful if the allergy is for things such as eggs or milk that are found in a wide range of foods, as you don't want to go to the trouble of avoiding them if it isn't necessary.

> 66 *My son switched from breastfeeding to formula at about the same time he started weaning. He started vomiting huge amounts and refused food so I became really anxious. My GP referred him to a paediatrician who said it was lactose intolerance but not to worry because he'd grow out of it. A dietitian friend gave me leaflets about introducing foods with lactose in. I followed the advice and now he's fine and can eat anything.* 99
> **Jo, mum to Samuel, 19 months**

There are great hopes for a cure being found at some point in the future and researchers are looking into it. One trial being carried out is trying to assess whether eating minute but increasing amounts of peanuts can build up the tolerance of children with a peanut allergy. However, for the time being, the only way to prevent allergic reactions is to carefully avoid the foods that your baby is allergic to. Some individuals need to avoid all traces of the food, but for others a small amount may be OK, or different forms of a particular food might be tolerated. For example, someone might have an allergic reaction if they drink milk, but they are fine if they eat a biscuit containing milk.

Living with an allergy

If your baby has been diagnosed with a food allergy, you will need to read the ingredients lists on food packaging very carefully. You might also want to receive 'Allergy Alerts'. These are warnings issued by the Food Standards Agency when a shop recalls a food product because it has been labelled wrongly. For example, a cake may be labelled as being milk-free, but milk has accidentally been added in the factory where it is produced.

TIP Go to the Food Standards Agency website (www.food.gov.uk) and sign up to have Allergy Alerts sent to you by email or SMS text. That way, if you have a wrongly labelled product at home, you will know not to give it to your baby.

In the past it was more difficult to buy food if you had an allergy, but many companies now manufacture products specifically for allergy sufferers. Most supermarkets also have 'free-from' ranges, which can make shopping easier. Any packaged food should be labelled with every ingredient it contains, even if it is only a very small amount. Since 2005, foods sold within the EU have been required by law to state on their label if they contain any of the 14 foods that are considered most likely to cause allergies: gluten, eggs, crustaceans, fish, peanuts, soya beans, milk, other nuts, celery, mustard, sesame seeds, sulphur dioxide and sulphides, molluscs and lupin. If the product contains any form of derivative of one of these foods, the label should also give the name of the food. For example, if a product contains whey powder it must say 'from cows' milk', so that those with a milk allergy find it easier to identify foods that they should avoid.

> TIP It's impossible to be sure about the ingredients of unpackaged products, such as bread from a bakery. To be on the safe side, it is best to assume that all bakery products contain eggs and milk.

If your baby has an allergy, or you suspect she does, it's easy to become anxious about everything she eats and start avoiding a whole range of foods 'just in case'. But this can result in your baby having a very limited diet, particularly if she's allergic to milk or eggs, which are found in lots of different foods. Living successfully with an allergy isn't just about knowing what to avoid. It is important to identify alternative foods so that your baby can enjoy a varied and nutritious diet. Babies with allergies are more likely than others to develop vitamin and mineral deficiencies. It is important to get specialist advice, and if your baby is on a very limited diet then blood tests for nutrient deficiencies may be necessary.

If your baby is at risk of having a severe allergic reaction, you may be given a pre-loaded adrenaline (epinephrine) injection kit to use in case a severe reaction occurs. These are known as EpiPens or Anapens. You may also be advised to carry medicine containing antihistamine, which you can give if your baby has a milder reaction. It is also a good idea for your baby or toddler to wear a MedicAlert bracelet.

There are several things you can do to keep your baby safe.

- Learn to read food labels carefully. As well as looking out for a particular food, you'll need to know about any alternative names.

- If your baby is allergic to a major food group, such as dairy products, see a Registered Dietitian or Registered Nutritionist to check she's getting all the nutrients she needs.
- Make sure your baby's nursery or anyone who looks after her has an action plan to cope with a reaction if it occurs.
- If you have an EpiPen, never go anywhere without it.
- Make sure anyone who might give your baby food, including restaurant staff, knows she has an allergy.
- Get lists from food companies and supermarkets about their products that are gluten-free, nut-free, egg-free, etc.
- Be prepared when eating out or going on holiday.
- Sign up to receive Allergy Alerts from the Food Standards Agency.

Here are some other tips.

- Experiment with different recipes or buy an allergy-free cookbook.
- Don't be afraid to try new foods.
- Get your baby re-tested to see if she's outgrown her allergy.

> 66 When I gave Hannah fromage frais for the first time she immediately screamed, her lips swelled and she vomited violently. Then she got very distressed, cried like someone was pressing on her voice box and her eyes swelled. I took her straight to the health clinic and things calmed down. We had many other weaning experiences that ended up in hospital but we've coped. Hannah's very sensible and she's outgrown some allergies. We're only now getting a comprehensive list of what she's allergic to. 99
> Louise, mum to Hannah, 7 years and Betty, 5 years

Milk allergy and intolerance

If your baby developed hives and swelling as soon as you gave her infant formula, you can be fairly certain she has cows' milk protein allergy (CMPA). CMPA can also result in eczema, reflux, colic, diarrhoea or constipation, and if she has these symptoms it is more difficult to get a diagnosis, as babies can have these for other reasons too. To complicate things even further, reactions to milk may be due to an intolerance rather than an allergy. A reaction to milk often occurs very early on when you first give milk, but not always. Problems like this can be difficult to diagnose, and an allergy expert is really the best person to tease out exactly what is going on.

An allergy to cows' milk sounds pretty much the same as an intolerance, but in fact these two conditions have different causes and they need to be handled differently.

What causes milk intolerance?

- Babies don't produce enough of the enzyme lactase.
- They can't break down lactose, which is the sugar found in all milk (including breast milk).
- Lactose passes into the small intestine where it ferments and produces gases and discomfort. Symptoms can also include diarrhoea and constipation.
- Sometimes lactose intolerance occurs temporarily following a bout of gastroenteritis. This can last for up to two to four weeks and should be treated in the same way as long-term intolerance.
- Sometimes babies can tolerate some milk, but they'll get symptoms if they have more than their body can digest.

How to treat milk intolerance

Before you start weaning

- If you're formula-feeding, switch from a regular formula to a lactose-free formula or a low-lactose formula.
- If you're breastfeeding, give your baby lactase (your GP or allergy specialist can advise you about products such as Colief).
- Cutting out milk from your own diet won't help, as your body produces lactose for your breast milk.

When you're weaning

- Try limiting the amount of milk you give at any one meal or feed.
- Give cows' milk or dairy foods as part of a mixed meal rather than on their own. This way they're digested more slowly.
- Instead of giving liquid milk, give hard cheese as this contains less lactose. Also try yogurt, which is generally better tolerated as it naturally contains the enzyme lactase.

What causes cows' milk protein allergy?

- A baby's immune system reacts against the proteins found in cows' milk.

How to treat cows' milk allergy

Before you start weaning

- If you're formula-feeding, switch to a hypoallergenic formula. The type you need depends on your baby's age and the specific type of reactions she has displayed. Some babies will do well with an extensively hydrolysed infant formula and others with an amino acid formula. However, if symptoms continue, then an elemental formula might be better. These can be prescribed by your GP.
- Sheep's milk or goats' milk is not usually suitable for babies with CMPA.
- Soya-based formulas are sometimes prescribed, particularly for older babies and those who are vegan. There was concern in the past about possible oestrogen-like effects, but research now suggests this is not something to worry about.
- If you're breastfeeding, you may need to avoid having cows' milk and any dairy products such as yogurt and cheese.

When you're weaning

- Use a hypoallergenic formula for cooking instead of cows' milk.
- If your baby doesn't like the taste of hypoallergenic formula, soya-based formulas are often more popular and may be worth a try.
- Avoid giving your baby milk, butter, cheese, yogurt, fish fingers and dairy ice cream.
- You'll also need to choose the following foods carefully as some brands (but not all) contain milk protein: margarine, biscuits, cakes, breakfast cereals and rusks.
- Avoid foods if the ingredients list shows they contain caseinate, caseinate salts, sodium caseinate, whey powder, whey protein, hydrolysed whey or whey syrup.
- Some babies who are allergic to cows' milk are OK if they have UHT milk rather than fresh milk. You can also try soya milk.
- Milk substitutes derived from oats or rice are not suitable as they don't provide enough protein, fat and other nutrients for growing babies. Organic varieties also lack calcium as they aren't fortified.

Rice milk should not be given either as it has been found to contain traces of arsenic.

If your baby is diagnosed with CMPA, it is reassuring to know there is a 50:50 chance she'll outgrow it before her first birthday. It is also estimated that 75% of babies outgrow CMPA by the age of two and 90% by the time they are three years old. Less than 1% go on to have a life-long milk allergy. If your baby was diagnosed with CMPA soon after being born, you may be advised not to introduce any cows' milk or dairy products until she reaches 12 months. Then you could slowly introduce a small amount, followed by larger quantities if no reaction occurs.

> 66 *Emily was breastfed until six months, then I gave her some formula and she immediately went bright red, had hives and was wheezy. It was obviously the formula, so I went straight to the GP, who thought it was a virus. I tried different formulas, but things got worse: projectile vomiting, diarrhoea, asthma, and she became as thin as a rake. At nine months, she had some egg and her mouth swelled. The sixth GP we saw referred her to an asthma and allergy consultant and tests showed she was allergic to milk and eggs. The hardest bit was dealing with all the barriers.* 99
> **Donna, mum to Katie, 12 years and Emily, 5 years**

Babies who can't have cows' milk can miss out on the nutrients that milk and dairy foods generally provide, including calcium, vitamin B12, fat and fat-soluble vitamins, particularly vitamin D. This means that if your baby is diagnosed with CMPA or milk intolerance, you will not only have to think about which foods to avoid, you'll also need to be more careful about ensuring she has an adequate nutrient intake. As part of your care, you should be able to see a dietitian who will be able to give you specific advice depending on exactly what your baby can and can't have. You might also find it helpful to look online for milk-free recipes. As well as looking at parenting or cookery sites, vegan websites might be helpful, as vegans don't consume any milk.

Egg allergy

Egg allergies vary in severity and type. An allergy to the proteins in egg white is more common than one to egg yolk, but both are possible, and some people are allergic to both egg yolk and white. Typically, symptoms, such as a rash and swelling, will occur within minutes of eating egg. But sometimes signs of a reaction will start an hour or more afterwards. If you suspect an allergy and see your doctor, a diagnosis may be made just on the basis of information you give about reactions.

If your baby has an egg allergy, some foods that need to be avoided are obvious, for example boiled and scrambled eggs, omelettes and quiche. Other foods that contain eggs can be harder to spot. For example, egg is sometimes used to glaze pastry products such as pies or biscuits. It is also found in products that are coated in breadcrumbs or batter, such as fish fingers.

> TIP Babies who are allergic to hens' eggs usually need to avoid eggs from other birds too, such as duck or turkey eggs.

Some people are allergic to all forms of egg. Others have a reaction to dishes like boiled or scrambled eggs, while being perfectly fine with products such as biscuits, cakes and Quorn, where the egg is well cooked. This is because prolonged cooking alters the structure of the proteins in egg so that they no longer cause a reaction for some individuals.

Foods that often contain egg

- Bakery products and desserts such as cakes, biscuits, doughnuts, pies, pancakes, bread-and-butter pudding, custard and ice cream
- Starchy foods such as pasta and noodles and also Yorkshire puddings and potato croquets
- Sweets, including marshmallows, nougat and some chocolate bars
- Sauces such as horseradish, mayonnaise, and some gravy granules
- Savoury food products such as sausages and burgers, including both meat and vegetarian versions (made from Quorn or soya)

- Foods coated in breadcrumbs or batter, such as fish fingers and chicken nuggets

While these products often contain egg, it is possible to get egg-free versions of most of them, so read the labels. As well as looking for eggs, egg white or egg yolk, be aware of ingredients made from eggs (albumin, livetin, ovoglobulin, ovalbumin, ovomucin, vitellin and ovovitellin). Lecithin – E322 – can also be made from eggs, although soya lecithin is often used now and this is egg-free.

An allergy to eggs is more common in children than in adults, and about half of babies with an egg allergy will grow out of it by the time they are three years old. Others may grow out of the allergy a little later, and most will have outgrown it by the time they are adults.

People with an allergy to eggs sometimes worry about eating chicken, but this doesn't contain the same proteins so it is safe to eat. If your baby has an egg allergy she could miss out on certain nutrients, including protein, vitamin E and essential fatty acids. Alternative sources of these nutrients include oily fish, for protein and essential fatty acids, and sunflower oil and leafy green vegetables for vitamin E.

Nut and seed allergies

Many parents worry about their baby having an allergic reaction to nuts, but only 1% to 2% of babies have a nut allergy. Like other food allergies, a nut allergy is more likely if there is a history of allergic-type conditions in the family, so most parents are worrying unnecessarily. However, as an allergy to nuts can result in anaphylactic shock, it does need to be taken very seriously. If your baby is allergic to peanuts, then she is more likely than other babies to be allergic to other nuts and sesame seeds.

Peanut allergy

In the past, the DoH advised parents not to give their baby any peanuts if there was a family history of allergies, eczema, asthma or hay fever. However, in 2009 it issued new advice, partly because of research which found that following the previous guidelines didn't reduce the risks.

The advice for all babies is now the same: foods containing peanuts can be introduced from six months, while whole nuts should be avoided until five years of age because of the risk of choking.

Since allergic reactions to peanuts can be so severe, parents of allergic children need to read food labels very carefully. Peanuts and peanut oil are used in biscuits, cakes, breakfast cereals, vegetarian dishes, salad dressings and Chinese and Thai dishes. Unrefined peanut oil is likely to contain peanut protein, so it should be avoided, but refined peanut oil, which is more commonly used, should be safe.

In the past 10 to 20 years, the number of children with peanut allergies has doubled and it is now thought to affect about one in every 70 children. An allergy to peanuts is typically discovered when a toddler is between one and two years old. While all allergies are troublesome, peanut allergies are a particular problem because they can occur when a person is exposed to just a tiny amount of peanut. Sometimes this can even be just a trace of peanut on another child's fingers. The other issue, which you are probably already aware of, is that allergic reactions to peanuts can be extremely serious.

Typically, a reaction to peanuts will start with the development of itchy blotches or bumps starting on the face and spreading to the rest of the body. Other symptoms can include a runny nose, sneezing, coughing or gagging, breathing problems and vomiting. Sometimes, although this is rare, a person will go into anaphylactic shock, which can be life-threatening if it isn't treated immediately.

> TIP If your baby is allergic to peanuts, she should wear a MedicAlert bracelet and anyone who looks after her must have immediate access to her EpiPen and know how to use it.

Whereas children often grow out of other allergies, it is estimated that about 80% of those with a peanut allergy will have it for life.

Sesame allergy

Allergies to sesame seeds have increased in recent years and, as with nut allergies, reactions are sometimes very sudden and severe. The increasing number of people showing allergic reactions could partly be due to the increasing use of sesame seeds and sesame oil.

Sesame seeds are found in many breads, rolls, crackers and breadsticks, including mixed-seed loaves and burger buns. They are also found in less obvious places, such as in houmous, tahini, falafel, veggie burgers and halvah. Sesame oil is used in some salad dressings and in Asian cooking. As the oil is usually unrefined, it still contains traces of protein, so it can still cause an allergic reaction.

Wheat allergy, coeliac disease and wheat sensitivity

There tends to be some confusion over the terms 'wheat allergy', 'coeliac disease' and 'wheat sensitivity'. A true allergy to wheat is thought to be very rare. Individuals with a wheat allergy can react not just to gluten, which is the main protein in wheat, but also to other wheat proteins. Therefore, if your baby is allergic to wheat, she will need to have a completely wheat-free diet.

Those who have coeliac disease react to foods containing gluten and to similar proteins found in barley, rye and oats. Therefore, they need a gluten-free diet, but they can still have other derivatives of wheat. Wheat sensitivity has only very recently been identified as a separate condition from the other two. Those with the condition are harder to identify and need to avoid eating wheat.

> 66 *About four months ago Tom started with diarrhoea and had up to 12 acrid nappies a day. My GP said cut out dairy and eggs but didn't suggest alternatives. Tom was a bit better but was losing weight. The paediatrician didn't help but a friend suggested wheat allergy and cutting that out seems to have worked. I can't get a proper diagnosis, but I can't get help, like a prescription for special formula, until I have one. I feel stuck in the middle of something that I have no control over, with a baby who has a massively limited diet and no one wants to help.* 99
> **Lesley, mum to Tom, 11 months**

Coeliac disease is sometimes referred to as an allergy, but it is really a bowel disease that only occurs when a person has gluten. In babies with coeliac disease, the lining of the small intestine becomes damaged when they eat gluten. This means nutrients can't be absorbed properly, which can result in nutritional deficiencies including anaemia. Unfortunately, signs of deficiencies can be difficult to spot, and other symptoms of coeliac disease are sometimes mistaken for other problems such as a virus.

Signs to look out for

Signs of coeliac disease include diarrhoea, a bloated tummy, irritability and muscle wasting, particularly on the arms and legs. Babies with coeliac disease might lose weight or stop putting it on, even though they were growing steadily before they had foods containing gluten. Doctors sometimes call this, rather alarmingly, 'failure to thrive'.

As the symptoms of coeliac disease can also result from other dietary or health problems, the condition can take a long time to diagnose. In some babies with coeliac disease, the symptoms are very mild, but in others they are more severe.

If you suspect your baby could have coeliac disease, it is important to see your GP for help; your GP can arrange for testing. Parents may take their baby to the doctor with sickness, bowel problems, slow weight gain or because they are generally unsettled and be told the cause is probably gastroenteritis. The symptoms of coeliac disease can be confused with those of milk intolerance, and without a proper diagnosis it is not advisable to start cutting foods out of your baby's diet. This is partly because, without expert help, you probably won't cut out all the gluten anyway. Also, you may be restricting your baby's diet and therefore her nutrient intake unnecessarily.

If symptoms persist, then it is best to get a referral to a gastroenterologist. Unfortunately, many parents find they have to be very persistent in order to get the expert help their baby needs.

If coeliac disease is diagnosed, a gluten-free diet will be needed for life, as it isn't something babies grow out of.

66 When Tilly first had bread, at about seven months, she had quite dramatic projectile vomiting. She started vomiting after milk feeds too and had very bad diarrhoea. I kept going back to the GP, saw a nutritionist, a paediatrician and had blood tests, but they didn't show anything. Then she started losing hair and stopped talking, so I really put my foot down and got a referral to a paediatric gastroenterologist. Tilly was two by then. The gastroenterologist suspected coeliac disease straight away and pushed us to have a biopsy, which confirmed it. Tilly's now much better – she's growing, talking and has lots of energy. **99**
Clare, mum to Neepha, 6 years, Tilly, 3 years and Eliza, 20 months

Where is gluten found?

Wheat is contained in lots of everyday foods, including bread, breakfast cereals, cakes and pasta, so whether your baby has a wheat allergy, coeliac disease or wheat sensitivity, all these foods should be avoided. Some foods labelled as wheat-free are made with other grains that contain gluten, so they are not always suitable. If your baby doesn't eat wheat it is important to make sure she doesn't miss out on calcium, iron, niacin and thiamin, which are usually added to wheat flour. Alternative starchy foods include potatoes, rice and products made from flour derived from corn, rice, buckwheat or millet.

There are lots of naturally gluten-free foods, including meat, fish, beans, fruit, vegetables, milk and most dairy products. However, processed versions of these foods, such as sausages or baked beans, may need to be avoided as they often contain wheat. Wheat is also often found in other foods, such as soups, sauces and ready meals, including commercially available baby foods.

Fortunately it is becoming increasingly easy to choose a gluten-free diet. Most supermarkets sell a whole range of suitable foods, including bread, pasta and breakfast cereal. The downside is that these can be very expensive. Foods that are gluten-free often say so on the label. The Coeliac Society offers lots of information about which foods to choose and regularly produces lists of gluten-free foods (see p217).

Allergies and intolerances to food additives

Parents are often very wary of food additives, but children are more likely to be allergic to specific foods than to particular additives.

Sulphite sensitivity is not considered an allergy by strict definition, but it can lead to the same type of reaction. Sulphur dioxide and sulphites are added to many food products as a preservative to prevent bacterial growth, as well as to prevent browning in foods such as dried apricots. When these foods are eaten, people who are hypersensitive can experience skin reactions or wheezing and breathing difficulties. Those who have asthma are particularly prone to having a reaction when they eat foods containing sulphites. If you suspect your baby might have asthma, you may choose to avoid foods containing sulphites.

Food additives containing sulphites may be labelled as E220 to E228, plus E150b and E150d. If foods contain any of these additives, under EU law, the product's label should say they contain sulphites. Foods that are likely to contain sulphites include mixed dried fruit and products that use mixed dried fruit as an ingredient, such as hot cross buns and rock cakes. Sulphites are also in dried apricots, dried apple, dried mango and glacé cherries, and foods that contain these, including dried fruit snack bars and cereal bars. Sulphur dioxide is also added to some fruit and vegetable juices.

Another additive that people are sometimes hypersensitive to is monosodium glutamate, commonly known as MSG but also labelled as E621. MSG is used as a flavour enhancer in foods like some Chinese dishes, flavoured noodles, gravy granules and flavoured crisps. Some individuals also appear to be hypersensitive to azo dyes, which are used as food colourings in some bakery products, sweets and drinks.

More information

If you are worried that your baby has a food allergy or intolerance, then, as well as seeing your GP, you might find the following organisations helpful.

Allergy UK
www.allergyuk.org
01322 619898
If you decide to pay for care privately, the Allergy UK website will help you find a local accredited allergy specialist.

The Anaphylaxis Campaign
www.anaphylaxis.org.uk
01252 542029

Coeliac UK
www.coeliac.org.uk
0845 305 2060

12

Other dietary problems

Reflux (bringing up food or acid)

Most babies bring up a bit of milk after a feed in the first few months of life. This is quite normal and is often referred to as positing. Reflux is something more than this, however, and usually involves a baby bringing back much more milk.

Why does it happen?

A small valve, known as the oesophageal sphincter, usually prevents the contents of the stomach coming back up the oesophagus. However, in babies with reflux the valve isn't strong enough to do its job properly yet. As a result, food mixed with stomach acids comes either part of the way or all the way back again. If it comes only part of the way your baby won't be sick, but she'll still be able to feel the acid, which can be quite painful. This pain, also known as heartburn, is quite common in pregnancy, and anyone who's suffered from it will be able to sympathise with their baby.

Most babies who experience reflux continue to grow normally, but it can still be distressing both for them and for you. The symptoms of milk allergy or intolerance can sometimes be mistaken for reflux, so this may need further investigation. If you notice blood in your baby's vomit, if she doesn't gain as much weight as expected or if you have other worries, see your doctor.

> 66 Mark suffered from reflux right from the beginning. None of the medications helped, they just made him horribly constipated. My GP wasn't much help, but I saw a private doctor who recommended weaning at four and a half months. This made such a difference and he really enjoyed it. I don't think the girls were ready at that age, but he was keen and opening his mouth. I found that if I gave him solids after a breastfeed it would help keep the milk down too. 99
> **Marta, mum to Louise, 4 years, Sophie, 2 years and Mark, 7 months**

What can you do about it?

If your baby suffers from reflux, she may be prescribed some form of medication to ease the symptoms. It can also help if you try to keep your baby as upright as possible after she has milk, and feed little and often, rather than giving large feeds. Thickened milk feeds can also help, and your health visitor should be able to give you information about this. Both specialist thickened feeds and formula thickener should be available on prescription, and you can also ask a pharmacist about ones that can be bought over the counter. Parents sometimes choose to thicken formula themselves with rusks or other products, but this isn't a good idea (see p12). Likewise, making formula thicker by adding extra powder is not advisable, as the formula is then too concentrated and contains too much sodium and other minerals for a baby's kidneys to cope with.

> TIP Some parents report that certain foods, such as bananas, stay down better than others, so it's worth experimenting to see if there is anything in particular that helps your baby.

The good news is that as babies grow older, most get better. It is estimated that although half of babies suffer from reflux in the first few months, only about 5% still have problems when they reach 10 months of age. Moving from a liquid diet to a more solid diet may be part of the reason why symptoms improve. Also, as babies get older, their muscles get stronger so they are able to sit up and the sphincter preventing reflux also works better. Parents are sometimes advised to wean sooner rather than later to relieve symptoms, and although this doesn't help all babies, some parents find it makes a big difference.

When you start to wean, baby rice is a good first food because it is fairly neutral compared with some fruits, which can be more acidic.

> 66 Darragh had dreadful reflux – he was constantly bringing up milk, so he was always hungry. I was advised to wean him at four months, but we've got allergies in the family, so I waited until five months. I don't think solids made any difference. He had very acidic vomit and he became anaemic too. He did gradually get better but I think it put him off acidic fruit for good. Even now he won't eat oranges. 99
> **Pauline, mum to Jude, 9 years, Darragh, 7 years and Erin, 4 years**

Constipation

Constipation can be a really miserable condition for your baby and it can leave her feeling very uncomfortable and irritable. There is no 'normal' pattern of bowel movements for babies, such as once a day, nor is it the case that any less means a baby is constipated. What is normal varies from one baby to the next. While most babies do a poo two to four times a day, others do one once every few days and they're fine. However, if your baby or toddler doesn't poo as often as usual, strains when she does, produces very little poo or very hard poos, these are signs of constipation.

There are usually other signs too, including passing smelly wind, tummy ache and irritability. When babies are constipated they often go off their food as well.

What can you do about it?

If your baby seems to be prone to constipation, then it may be better to start weaning with some fruit, such as pear, rather than giving baby rice as a first food.

If constipation develops once your baby is eating solids, then changing her diet slightly may help make things better. The first thing to do is make sure dehydration isn't a problem. Babies can be prone to constipation if they reduce their milk intake but other fluids don't replace it. If you can see yellow marks in her nappy caused by urine, this is a sign that she needs more water. If she doesn't like drinking water, then don't be tempted to give her more formula, as this can make things worse. Formula milk contains substances that form what are called 'stool soaps', which make poos harder. Also, if your baby has lots of milk she won't have as much fruit and vegetables as she needs, which can make matters worse. Babies under a year shouldn't be having more than 500–600ml of milk per day and one to two-year-olds need no more than 350ml per day.

TIP Sometimes switching from a basic milk formula to a follow-on formula can result in constipation, and if this is the case the best thing to do is simply switch back again. Changing from breast milk to formula can also make constipation more likely, but it might help if you make the transition slowly. Choosing a formula that contains a probiotic may also be useful.

---

66 *Thomas was breastfed and would fill his nappy all day long until he started solids. Then he started on baby rice and didn't do a poo for about four days and we ended up calling the health visitor. He was quite chubby and hardly moved, which probably didn't help, and he wouldn't drink water, unless it was from a teaspoon or a china cup. Pears and prunes seemed to get things moving a bit, but he was constipated for a couple of months really.* 99
Paul, dad to Thomas, 10 months

Although extra milk isn't the answer, increasing a baby's intake of other fluids can help relieve constipation. Offering plenty of water, all day long, is the first thing to try, to get your baby drinking as much as possible. Much of the weight of a stool is water, and if a baby doesn't drink enough water or get enough of it from the foods she eats, this can lead to hard stools. To produce soft stools that are easier to pass requires a good intake of fluids. Every meal should be matched with a drink of water, and another cup of water should be offered between meals. If your baby has reached the stage of eating three meals and two snacks each day, then she should be having six to eight drinks as well. Increasing a baby's water intake isn't usually very easy, especially in the early days of weaning when most babies aren't used to it. Perseverance really is the key though, and if your baby won't drink water, there are plenty of tactics you can use to try to increase her intake (see p194).

As well as increasing the amount of fluids she has, you can look at the foods your baby is eating. Some people believe that certain foods, including bananas, rice and potatoes, can cause constipation. There is no scientific evidence to support this, but that doesn't mean your individual baby doesn't become more constipated when she eats a particular food.

Fruit

While avoiding certain foods may only help on an individual basis, many people find that increasing their baby's intake of fruit and vegetables does seem to get things moving. The fruits in the list below are the best ones to try first, but any fruit will help, as they all contain a large proportion of water.

Fruits that help with constipation

Apricots	Plums
Peaches	Raspberries
Pears	Strawberries
Prunes	

Prunes

If other fruits don't seem to work, then prunes might do the trick. Prunes are well known for their natural laxative effect, which is due to their high sorbitol content. This is a sugar that is absorbed very slowly and can pass into the large intestine. Prunes also contain phenolic compounds, which can have a laxative effect.

The simplest way to get your baby to eat prunes is to buy tinned ones, mash them with a fork and offer them as they are. They are naturally very sweet and your baby may well be happy to eat them. Otherwise you can try mixing them with yogurt or other fruits, such as apple purée or mashed banana. You can also buy a bottle of prune juice and try adding this to mashed fruit or porridge.

> **TIP** As prune juice usually comes in large bottles, it's a good idea to freeze some in ice-cube trays so that you can use small quantities when it's needed.

Probiotics and prebiotics

In recent years there has been an increasing amount of interest in the role of probiotics and prebiotics in regulating bowel habits. Research has shown that babies who are constipated have a different pattern of bacteria in their intestines than those without constipation.

One small study in Italy found that it helped to give babies with chronic constipation a particular probiotic (*Lactobacillus reuteri*). Babies taking the probiotic increased their average number of bowel movements a week from about three to five. The effects of giving babies probiotics aren't widely known and different strains are likely to produce different effects. So, if you want to try them, it's best to talk to your doctor first.

> 66 *Ella became constipated as soon as she started solids, and when she was a year the paediatrician put her on medication for chronic constipation. She's always had plenty of fruit, vegetables and fluids but I think it's a genetic thing. There's still a lot of guilt involved though. Prunes don't help, but I found acidophilus, the probiotic, is good and a multivitamin syrup with flaxseed oil. There's no solution that will help everyone, so I think it's trial and error to find what works for you.* 99
> **Ann, mum to Finn, 4 years and Ella, 2 years**

Fibre

With adults, the first dietary change recommended for constipation is to increase fibre intake. This means eating plenty of high-fibre foods such as wholemeal bread and pasta, brown rice, and breakfast cereals with added bran, such as bran flakes and All-Bran.

However, high-fibre foods, especially those with added bran, aren't good for babies because they are too bulky and reduce mineral absorption (see p28). It's good to get babies used to having wholemeal bread and other 'brown' products some of the time, but it's best *not* to offer these with every meal.

Fibre helps to relieve constipation by bulking up stools, so they can move through the intestines more easily. However, they do this by absorbing water, and if the problem is caused by a lack of fluids, then extra fibre can make things worse rather than better.

Exercise

Physical activity, including going for a walk, can help toddlers, older children and adults with constipation. As babies can't walk yet this obviously isn't a possibility, but you can still encourage your baby to move as much as possible, even if it's just rolling around or bouncing on your lap. You can also leave her nappy off for a while when she's on the changing mat so that she can have a good kick around. Or give her a longer bath than usual if she enjoys having a kick and splash there.

Allergies

Bear in mind that severe constipation that doesn't respond to normal dietary changes can sometimes be due to an allergy. It is true that allergic reactions are more usually associated with diarrhoea, but constipation can also be a symptom. If your baby has recently had a new food, then it's worth keeping a diary of her diet and any symptoms to see whether there is a connection.

Psychological issues

Sometimes constipation can become a partly psychological problem for a baby. If your baby has had trouble passing stools in the past, then she may become stressed when she feels she needs to go. You can help this by being relaxed yourself and gently massaging your baby's tummy to make things easier.

Psychological factors can also affect toddlers around the time of potty training and make constipation more likely. To avoid this it's important to keep a positive approach to potty training and avoid negative comments about smells or anything else. Sitting on the potty for five to 10 minutes is also important as this is long enough for a toddler to go but not so long that it becomes a nuisance for her.

Treatment for constipated babies who are eating solids

- Plenty of fluids, especially water
- Lots of fruit and vegetables
- Prunes or prune juice with food
- Not too much milk
- Exercise
- Laxatives if necessary

For many cases of mild constipation, extra fluids and a few dietary changes do the trick. Unfortunately, however, some babies and children are just more prone to constipation than others. They might eat and drink all the right things but still have a problem. If this is the case for your baby, then it's important to take her to see your GP or health visitor for help. Constipation can affect a baby's well-being and it needs to be sorted out. The worst thing to do is nothing.

> 66 *If your child has constipation, don't let anyone tell you they'll grow out of it because they won't. It needs to be tackled straight away so that things don't get worse. The NICE guidance document explains how the problem should*

be handled and it's useful for parents to look at, as well as health professionals. **99**
Dr Jenny Gordon, Programme Manager, Evidence into Practice, Royal College of Nursing, and chair of NICE guidance on the diagnosis and management of childhood constipation[3]

Laxatives

If you've tried other approaches already, your GP may recommend a laxative. Bulk-forming laxatives are not usually suitable for babies, but your GP may prescribe an osmotic laxative, which increases the fluid in the intestines and softens the stools.

You might not be keen to give your baby medication, but if her bowels have become impacted with hard stools, this may be the only way to remove the blockage. Then you can ensure she has a constipation-friendly diet to try to prevent the problem happening again. In some cases laxatives are only needed until a regular bowel habit is established, but in other cases long-term medication is needed.

Anaemia

Many babies and toddlers have low iron intakes and as a result anaemia is thought to be fairly common. The real number of babies affected isn't known, as a proper diagnosis requires a blood test and these aren't usually carried out unless there is a good reason to do so. However, a study carried out on a group of babies in South West England suggested that as many as one in five were affected. This may be an overestimate of the problem, but other studies of older children, including nationwide figures for pre-schoolers, show that a significant number of this age group also suffer from anaemia.

Babies with anaemia have low levels of haemoglobin, which is the molecule in red blood cells that carries oxygen. As a result, their blood has fewer red blood cells and the red cells that they do have are smaller. This means the blood can't carry as much oxygen around the body for energy production and normal functioning.

How to spot anaemia

The most typical signs of anaemia are pale skin and tiredness. Other signs include brittle nails, swollen tongue, irritability, feeling cold, poor appetite and frequent infections. However, it's also common for babies with anaemia not to show any obvious signs.

What causes anaemia?

The most common cause of anaemia is iron deficiency, and iron deficiency anaemia is the kind that is dealt with here. However, anaemia can also be caused by a lack of vitamin B12, and there are other types of anaemia that are inherited, such as sickle cell anaemia.

If it is suspected that your baby is suffering from anaemia, she will be given a blood test, which measures several different factors in the blood, including the level of haemoglobin, the number of red blood cells and the size of the red blood cells. It is necessary to look at these different measurements in order to find out if a person has anaemia and, if so, what kind of anaemia they have.

Reasons for babies becoming anaemic

- Not enough iron in the diet, e.g. a vegetarian diet and no foods fortified with iron
- Having too much milk instead of iron-rich foods (see p166)
- Delayed weaning beyond six months
- Too many foods that reduce iron absorption, e.g. tea, high-fibre foods and milk products
- Not enough foods that increase iron absorption, e.g. vitamin C-rich fruits and vegetables
- Long-term internal blood loss, for example in the oesophagus due to severe reflux or in the intestines due to other digestive problems
- Inadequate iron absorption due to coeliac disease
- Being born with low iron stores due to premature birth

What are the effects of anaemia?

Iron deficiency anaemia results in an inadequate supply of oxygen to the body's tissues, which affects energy production. As a result, babies and toddlers with anaemia can seem lethargic and lacking in energy.

If anaemia isn't treated, it can cause developmental delays and have long-term effects on brain development. Anaemia can also affect the immune system, leading to more frequent illnesses.

Treating anaemia with diet

The amount of iron that is available for a baby to absorb in her intestines depends largely on the amount of iron that is in the food she eats. It is also affected by the foods eaten at the same time that increase or reduce absorption. So each of these factors needs to be targeted.

- Increase iron intake. Pre-schoolers get most of the iron in their diet from cereal products. Giving a breakfast cereal with added iron every morning is an easy way to boost intake. Other iron-rich foods you can give your baby include meat, fish, beans, peanut butter and other nut butter and dried fruit, such as apricots and raisins. (A dried apricot contains no more than a fresh one, but because it contains less water the iron is more concentrated.)
- Have more foods that increase absorption. This means more high-vitamin C foods, such as kiwi, oranges, strawberries, broccoli and tomatoes. These need to be eaten at the same meal as the iron-rich foods mentioned above to have an effect.
- Eat fewer foods that reduce absorption. This means no tea, coffee or cereals with added bran.
- Don't have more milk than is needed, then your baby's intake of solids will increase.

Babies who drink cows' milk instead of breast milk or formula are more likely to become anaemic. Cows' milk contains less iron and it is more difficult for babies to absorb. Also, it can irritate the lining of a baby's intestines. Additionally, babies who are breastfed may be more prone to anaemia than formula-fed babies, as formula contains more iron than breast milk, although it is in a form that is more difficult for a baby's body to absorb. Sometimes mums who are breastfeeding are advised to give their baby some formula to boost iron intake, but according to NICE there is no evidence that this is effective.

Iron supplements

If your baby has blood tests and the results show she is anaemic, your doctor will be able to prescribe a suitable iron supplement. This should be taken alongside treatment with dietary measures. Some parents decide to give their baby a supplement just to be on the safe side, since there is so much concern about deficiency. However, this is not recommended and there is some evidence that taking supplements when iron levels are normal can cause problems. If you want to boost your baby's iron intake as a precautionary measure, the best way to do this is with diet.

13

Premature babies

If your baby was born prematurely you may have particular concerns about when to start weaning and how to go about introducing solids. Although some 7% of children born in the UK are delivered prematurely (before week 37 of pregnancy), there are no official guidelines about introducing solids to these babies. Your healthcare professionals will be the best people to give you advice, based on how premature your baby was and her general growth and health. However, it can also be helpful and reassuring to get some general information too.

When to start weaning

The government guidelines on the introduction of solids from about six months are intended for healthy full-term babies. The official advice regarding premature babies is that they should be dealt with individually.

> TIP Experts from Bliss, the charity for premature babies, recommend weaning somewhere between five and eight months after birth. In general it's thought that the earlier a baby was born, the later she should begin weaning.

There is no need to wait until six months after your baby's original due date, as many of the organ systems develop more rapidly following a premature delivery than if your baby had remained in the womb for longer, which you probably wouldn't expect.

Premature babies have additional nutrient requirements, as they didn't have as long in the womb to build up stores of iron and other nutrients. Some experts suggest that premature babies need to be weaned earlier than others to ensure an adequate intake of essential nutrients. To test whether there is any benefit in early weaning, research was carried out with premature babies admitted to the Royal Hampshire County Hospital. Half the parents in the study were advised to wean their babies from 13 weeks after birth (approximately three months), and the other half to follow the standard weaning advice, which at the time was to wean from 17 weeks (four months). The babies who were weaned early were also given meals that were more nutrient dense than normal weaning foods, and together these factors appeared to be beneficial. The babies grew faster in length and they had better iron levels. This study was carried out about 10 years ago, and the general consensus now seems to be that three months is probably too early for most babies to start weaning. However, the nutrient-dense diet that was used may be beneficial and we look at this later (see p233).

The advice from Bliss is that it is best to wait until at least three months after your baby's due date before you start introducing solids. This means if your baby was born at 34 weeks, you should wait until she is about four and a half months old, but if she was born at 30 weeks then it might be better to wait until she reaches at least five and half months. This is partly because she will then be physically better able to manage. For example, she will have better head control and be able to sit up straighter. Her hand–eye co-ordination will also be more developed.

If you start to wean very much before your baby is three months beyond her due date, it might also affect her risk of developing allergies. Just as very early weaning increases the risk of allergic-type conditions in full-term babies, so it does with premature babies. One research study, carried out in South East England, found that it was better to wait until babies were at least 10 weeks past their due date before starting weaning. It was shown that in families with no history of allergic-type conditions, this reduced the babies' risk of developing eczema.

As you can see, the advice isn't clear-cut and there isn't an exact age at which it is best to start weaning. When deciding the best time to begin weaning your baby, you will have to weigh up the benefits of faster catch-up growth against the possible risks of allergies. It's also important to consider whether your baby is showing any interest in food and to think about the usual signs that a baby is ready for weaning (see p11).

> **66** My twins were born eight weeks premature and, on the advice of my health visitor, I started weaning at four months [from their birth date]. From the start, they both had a great appetite. They also started sleeping better and they seemed more content during the day. I've learned from this to have confidence in what you think is right for your babies, based on the signs they are giving you, rather than blindly following the general NHS advice. It is good advice, but it isn't always the best for every single baby. **99**
> **Zara, mum to Ciara and Ruairi, 3 years**

What foods to give

All babies, including those born early, need foods from the different food groups for healthy growth and development (see p14). However, premature babies have extra energy needs, and also require more protein, iron, zinc, calcium, selenium and long-chain polyunsaturates. In the early days, most of these needs are met by breast milk or a special preterm infant formula.

When you begin weaning, it's good to start with vegetables and fruit, just as you would with a baby born at full term. However, these foods are generally low in calories and protein, so giving them on their own may not be suitable.

Premature babies can also be very sensitive to the volume of food and drink they consume. So when they start having solids, they are likely to take less milk to compensate. If those solids are fruit and vegetables, it means they will be having a lower energy and protein intake overall. However, if you are aware of these issues, it is possible to get round them.

In the study mentioned earlier, carried out with premature babies in Hampshire, parents were given the following advice about feeding their babies.

- Foods should contain at least 70–105 kcal per 100g.
- Cereals and savoury foods should contain 2.3–5.0g of protein per 100g.
- Fruit puddings and other desserts should contain 1.0–4.0g of protein per 100g.
- Preterm formula milk should be used in home cooking and to make up cereals.

If you are buying commercially prepared baby food, these guidelines might be useful for you to compare with the nutrient content list on the product.

If you are making your own baby food, it's impossible to know the exact calorie or protein content of meals. However, a few simple strategies may be helpful.

- Mix fruit purées with baby rice.
- Mix vegetables with a starchy food, such as baby rice or potato (or, when your baby is old enough, pasta or other wheat-based foods).
- Include higher-calorie fruit and vegetables, such as bananas and avocados, with lower-calorie ones like pears, carrots and broccoli.
- Mix peas and beans, which contain more calories and protein, with other vegetables.
- If you are buying jars or pouches of baby food for pudding, try fruity breakfasts instead as these often have cereals added too.
- When your baby starts having meat, fish and alternatives, give these twice a day.
- When you're cooking, don't skimp on the vegetable oil or margarine, as this is an easy way to increase calories without adding bulk.
- Use preterm formula rather than water or regular formula for making cereal, mashed potato or other dishes than need extra liquid.

> ## Cows' milk
>
> Most babies can have cows' milk as their main drink from 12 months of age. However, formula-fed babies who were premature may benefit from delaying the switch until 15 to 18 months.

Supplements

A supplement containing vitamins A, D and E is important for all babies (see p16). Premature babies may also need supplements containing other vitamins and minerals, due to their lack of nutrient stores. Babies' stores of iron in particular build up during the last 12 weeks of pregnancy, and this typically lasts them for the first six months of life. Iron deficiency typically occurs from six months onwards in full-term babies; however, premature babies are at risk earlier, during the first six months of life. Iron deficiency in premature babies can affect growth and brain development, so it's particularly important to treat it.

Those who are breastfed are at particular risk as preterm formula has extra iron added to make up for the baby's extra need. However, not all premature babies need iron supplements: those who've had repeated blood transfusions, for example, can end up with iron overload if they also have a high iron intake, so you need to talk to your specialist.

How to feed your baby

Follow the basic information for all babies given in Chapter 1 of this book.

Whether baby-led weaning (BLW) is a suitable option for your baby really depends on her individual growth and development. Some premature babies can be weaned just like babies born at full term, but others require a little bit more help. It may be that your baby needs more food than she is capable of feeding herself at the beginning, so it might be better to do some spoon-feeding.

> TIP Your baby will probably need purées to start with, but give her finger foods too as soon as she's ready to eat them.

Slow feeding can be more common in premature babies, so lots of patience is needed. It can mean that the process of moving from smooth purées to lumps can take longer and your baby may take a little while to move from one meal to two and then three. This may be another reason why it's better to start weaning earlier, and then the need to move on isn't so pressing. If your baby has problems moving on to lumps, then take it slowly, but do persevere and try not to be overly cautious. If you're worried about your baby's eating, do ask for help. If you feel you need specialist help, ask for a referral to a paediatric dietitian or a speech and language therapist (who can help with advice on swallowing and other mouth-related issues).

Parents of premature babies are sometimes particularly worried about their baby developing allergies, but there is no evidence that babies born early are at any greater risk than full-term babies. One problem that is more common, however, is constipation; if this is the case for your baby, follow the advice on p220.

> 66 Leon was born two months early and he actually instigated weaning himself when he was about six months. I was eating a banana, he grabbed my hand, pulled it towards him and started eating. Then he carried on feeding himself but he had purées too. I did freestyle cooking – using Annabel Karmel as a starting point but figuring out new recipes he might like. He's caught up with other kids and at the moment he loves pasta and anything he can feed himself. 99
> **Tim, dad to Leon, 19 months**

> TIP For more information contact Bliss at www.bliss.org.uk or on their freephone support helpline 0500 618 140.

14

Vegetarian babies

If you are a vegetarian, you are probably already aware of the health benefits of vegetarianism. People who don't eat meat or fish tend to have a higher intake of fruit and vegetables and a reduced risk of obesity, bowel cancer and heart disease.

Despite these health benefits, you may have come across concern from other people, such as grandparents or health professionals, when you mention bringing up your baby as a vegetarian. These worries are not completely unfounded, as you will need to be careful about what you feed your baby, and pay particular attention to energy, protein and iron intake. However, you can reassure any worriers that your baby will be able to enjoy a very healthy and well-balanced diet. With a few small tweaks, it should be possible to adapt most of the meals you eat yourself so that they are suitable for your baby.

The nutrients that you particularly need to look out for are listed below, along with some ideas about how to ensure your baby's diet contains sufficient amounts. If you are feeding your baby a lacto-ovo-vegetarian (LOV) diet, which includes milk products and eggs, it is easier to plan a nutritionally complete diet. However, if your baby is vegan (no milk or eggs or any other foods of animal origin), then more careful meal planning is required. Vegan babies, and also LOVs who don't eat many dairy products, are at greater risk of having inadequate intakes of calcium and vitamin B12, as dairy foods are usually a major source of these micronutrients.

> 66 *Healthy, happy children have been raised without meat for thousands of years. My health visitor was great about us being a vegetarian family. She once said that as a veggie who paid attention to what I ate myself, I knew more about keeping my children healthy than most of the mothers she met.* 99
> **Liz, mum to Laurence, 6 years and Orla, 3 years**

As well as looking at particular nutrients, this chapter describes how to feed your baby at each stage of weaning. As you'll see, there is nothing you need to do differently at the beginning, as most babies start with fruit, vegetables and cereals anyway. As weaning progresses and babies require more nutrients from food and fewer from milk, you will need to think carefully about providing a varied and nutrient-dense diet. On the whole, you'll find that, when it comes to weaning your vegetarian baby, there are more similarities with weaning a non-vegetarian baby than differences. Most of the information throughout the book is still relevant to you. This chapter just covers the little extra bits of information you need to know.

Food types and nutrients to be aware of

Protein

Your baby needs a variety of protein-rich foods to ensure she gets essential amino acids and other essential nutrients.

There is a variety of foods that can supply a vegetarian baby with protein:

- well-cooked eggs
- full-fat milk
- full-fat cheeses
- full-fat yogurt and fromage frais
- beans, including kidney, cannellini and haricot beans

- chickpeas, including houmous and falafel
- lentils, including in dhal, pasta sauce or pâté
- nuts, in the form of smooth nut butters and ground nuts (whole nuts only for over-fives)
- seeds (these are best ground, for example in tahini)
- soya, including tofu
- Quorn – this is high in protein but, as it is a low-fat food, you could use extra oil in cooking to compensate
- wheat protein – as well as being found in wheat products such as bread, this is sometimes used in vegetarian products like sausages
- cereals, such as corn, wheat and rice – these also supply protein.

By the time your baby is about seven months old, she will need to be eating at least one portion of a protein-rich food, such as lentils or eggs, every day. This should increase to two portions a day by the time she is nine months old. Foods such as beans, nuts and seeds can be hard for a baby's digestive system to break down. So if you give these foods to your baby, you may well notice when you change her nappy that they come out pretty much in the same state as they went in. You can help the process along, and make the nutrients more easily available to your baby, if you mash beans and lentils before giving them. Also, choose smooth nut butters rather than crunchy ones, as even small pieces of nut are hard to break down further in order to release the nutrients.

Babies need proportionately more protein for their size than adults. So when you are sharing family meals, such as a stew made with beans, vegetables and potatoes, make sure your baby gets plenty of the beans. You could also consider mixing a spoonful of nut butter into your baby's portion. This is a very easy way to increase the fat, protein and iron content.

> TIP If you're cooking something a bit spicy, such as a mild curry or chilli, you could mix a spoonful of full-fat Greek yogurt into your baby's portion to add extra fat and reduce the spiciness at the same time.

Convenience foods for vegetarians, such as vegetarian sausages and veggie burgers, are often quite high in salt. Vegetarian sausages, just like their meaty counterparts, can contain nearly 1g of salt each, which is the maximum amount a baby should have in a day. If you buy foods like these, it's best to compare labels, as some brands are better than others.

> TIP If you usually eat vegetarian sausages or burgers, try making them yourself instead. Or just make a batch for your baby and keep them in the freezer. Then she can have one of these when you're having a shop-bought version.

> 66 *My husband, who eats meat, was a little concerned about giving a vegetarian diet. Once I provided him with nutrition information from the Vegetarian Society and reassured him vegetarian children can grow up healthily, he supported me 100%. We worry about everything as parents and sometimes it's challenging to get them to eat anything at all. I try not to stress about it and I find talking to other veggie mums is invaluable.* 99
> **Georgia, mum to Josie, 2 years and expecting her second baby in 3 months**

Omega 3 fatty acids

Oily fish is the main source of long-chain omega 3 fatty acids, which are beneficial for a baby's brain and eye development (see p18). Some vegetarians decide to include these in their baby's diet occasionally, but if you don't want to do this, then including more short-chain omega 3 fatty acids may be beneficial. These are found in foods such as flaxseed oil, rapeseed oil and walnuts. It is best to use flaxseed oil cold, in salad dressings or dips, as the fatty acids can become damaged when it is heated.

Iron

Vegetarian babies are particularly vulnerable to anaemia. This is because iron is found in meat and fish in the form of haem iron, which is more readily absorbed by the body than non-haem iron from plant foods. To ensure your baby has high enough iron levels you need to look at the amount of iron she is eating but also at her intake of foods that increase or reduce iron absorption.

Good sources of iron for vegetarians include:

- dried fruit such as apricots (soaked and puréed)
- beans and lentils
- cereal products, particularly breakfast cereals with added iron.

The amount of iron absorbed can be increased if these foods are eaten with vitamin C (see p17), and it is reduced if iron-rich foods are eaten with tea or high-fibre foods. Vegetarians tend to have a higher vitamin C intake than non-vegetarians, but to ensure that the vitamin C helps with iron absorption it's essential that these nutrients are eaten at the same time.

Some vegetarians prefer to choose food that is organically produced and less processed. While food in its natural state is generally healthier, it may benefit your baby to have a lower-fibre breakfast cereal with added vitamins and minerals.

Calcium and vitamin D

If you are bottle-feeding your baby and she is taking 500–600ml of milk per day, you can be sure she is getting enough calcium. Likewise, if you are breastfeeding, your baby should also be getting all the calcium she needs. Remember to have plenty of calcium-rich foods yourself though, as it is important for your own health.

There is no need for your baby to have more than about five breastfeeds or 600ml of formula per day. Having more milk than this can mean your baby misses out on the other nutrients she needs, including iron (see p166).

If you are bringing up your baby as a vegan or if she is an LOV but is not having much milk, then it is best to talk to a health professional about ensuring an adequate nutrient intake. If your baby doesn't have any milk, she could be at risk of multiple nutrient deficiencies.

Vitamin B12

Vitamin B12 is found in milk, and your baby should get enough from breast milk or formula. However, as she gets older and consumes less milk, ensuring an adequate intake can become a problem.

As vitamin B12 isn't found naturally in foods of plant origin, it can be completely missing from vegan diets. Most vegans compensate for this by having foods (such as soya milk) that are fortified with the vitamin. If you plan to give foods like this to your baby, you should be aware that not all soya milks are fortified with vitamin B12 or calcium. This includes organic soya milk, as organic certification doesn't allow this fortification. Most soya milks also lack fat and other nutrients found in cows' milk.

Fibre

Vegetarians tend to eat more fibre than non-vegetarians, which is an advantage for adults as high-fibre diets are associated with lower rates of constipation and bowel problems, including irritable bowel syndrome (IBS). However, a high-fibre diet isn't suitable for babies, as it is bulky and reduces the absorption of iron and zinc, which may be limited in vegetarian diets already.

Your baby will probably be getting enough fibre from the fruit, vegetables and pulses she eats, so it may be better to give her white pasta and rice rather than wholegrain versions. Also, some breakfast cereals, such as high-fibre muesli, aren't suitable. As mentioned earlier, while it is great for babies to join in family meals, a balanced approach is best, and a different breakfast cereal may be beneficial to ensure an adequate nutrient intake. If you choose a cereal such as Weetabix or an own-brand equivalent (though not organic versions), you'll still be providing wholegrain wheat. The advantage over high-fibre muesli is that it doesn't have added bran fibre and it is fortified with iron. As your baby gets older, you can mix it with dried fruit and ground nuts to boost the nutrient content even further.

> 66 Both my daughters have thrived on their vegetarian diet. My mother-in-law (who is very much non-vegetarian) commented about how healthy they are compared to their non-vegetarian cousins. My only concern has been regarding omega 3s from oily fish, and I gave my eldest tinned salmon a couple of times, but I didn't feel comfortable about it. I think it's important for all parents to present a positive attitude about food to their baby, eat with them and have the same food. 99
> **Susan, mum to Kiri, 4 years and Julia, 2 years**

Stages of weaning

Stage 1 (four to six months)

When you start to wean your baby you can offer fruit and vegetables in just the same way as you would for a non-vegetarian baby. Before about six or seven months, there is no real difference, and the advice for stage 1 is exactly the same for vegetarians and non-vegetarians alike (see Chapter 6).

Stage 2 (seven to nine months)

As babies move on to the second stage of weaning, they need to have a more diverse diet and to eat protein foods regularly. Milk is still an important source of nutrients, but your baby will need to eat something from the list of protein-rich foods every day. As well as providing protein foods, you should think about introducing lumpy foods and finger foods at this stage.

Most of the recipes and food ideas described in Chapter 7 for stage 2 are suitable for vegetarians. Ideal meals for vegetarian babies include dishes such as tomato medley (see p138), which is a good source of iron, and carrot and coriander mash (see p139), which includes well-cooked lentils. You can also incorporate lentils, mashed tofu and mashed beans and peas into pasta sauces and stews.

Most babies will need some help to eat foods like this, even if it's just a case of loading their spoon with dishes such as carrot and coriander mash. If you are keen to follow baby-led weaning (BLW), you may not want to do this, but it is important to consider nutrient requirements. If you want to stick to finger foods, then an omelette is a good option. You could also give pieces of vegetable, such as broccoli florets, dipped in houmous or lemony lentil dip (see p155). With foods like this, keep an eye on how much is actually eaten and how much is wasted. Soon your baby will be able to manage feeding herself foods like this, but she might need help at this stage.

66 *I wasn't overly worried about feeding Kieran a vegetarian diet, as I've been vegetarian for many years and know the areas I need to think about. I found a good way of*

introducing protein was whizzing up lentils or other pulses and mixing them with his food. The early stage of weaning wasn't too difficult, but I sometimes had to mix fruit with vegetables to get him to eat them and he gagged on lumps. He's turned out to be a fussy eater, but it's best to stay calm – they somehow still manage to get what they need from the limited foods they eat! **99**
Vicky, mum to Kieran, 2 years

Stage 3 (nine to 12 months)

In the third stage of weaning, your baby should be getting used to eating a really good range of foods and joining in family meals as much as possible. With vegetarian babies, it is particularly important that a variety of different foods is eaten, particularly different protein-rich foods, but also a range of starchy foods. This increases the likelihood that they are having all the essential nutrients. Your baby should be eating two portions of protein-rich foods a day. Try to make sure these aren't just cheese, as this provides the same nutrients as the milk she is already having. Instead, try to include different foods from the list on p237.

Finger foods become increasingly popular at this stage and dips such as houmous and dhal can be included with pitta and vegetables to make a healthy meal. Nut butters are also good for spreading on rice cakes or toast.

Toddlers and beyond

As your baby becomes a toddler, she will hopefully join in family meals even more. To ensure meals aren't too salty, you can flavour them with low-salt stock cubes and yeast extract without added salt, as well as using herbs and spices. Your baby will still need a higher-fat and lower-fibre diet than you for at least the next year. Then, if she's healthy and growing well, you can start to slowly adapt what she eats so that by the age of five she's having the type of diet that would be considered healthy and balanced for a vegetarian adult.

Further information

The Vegetarian Society provides lots of useful information on its website, including how to feed babies and children and easy recipes for family meals (www.vegsoc.org). You can also call them on 0161 925 2000, from 8.30am to 5pm, Monday to Friday. The Society also has a mentor scheme for members.

The Vegan Society also provides information and advice. The website is www.vegansociety.com and you can also call them on 0121 523 1730, from 9am to 5pm, Monday to Friday.

Index

Endnotes

1 Baird, J. *et al.*, 'Being big or growing fast: systematic review of size and growth in infancy and later obesity', *British Medical Journal*, vol.331, no.7522, pp.929–31.

2 Dangour, A. D. *et al.*, 'Nutritional quality of organic foods: a systematic review', *American Journal of Clinical Nutrition*, vol.90(3), pp.680–5.Dangour, A. D. et al., 'Nutrition-related health effects of organic foods: a systematic review', *American Journal of Clinical Nutrition*, vol.92(1), pp.203–10.

3 The NICE guidance on the diagnosis and management of childhood constipation can be found on the NICE website at http://guidance.nice.org.uk/CG99.